江苏大学国家级一流专业"英语"专业建设成果
国家社会科学基金项目（16BWW014）的阶段性成果

English Translation of Poems from the Tang and Song Dynasties
唐宋诗撷英新译

万雪梅
［美］弗雷德里克·特纳（Frederick Turner）　编　译

东南大学出版社
·南京·

内容提要

本书精选了不同流派、不同风格的唐宋诗共159首,在充分研读的基础上,在尽量不改变原诗意思的基础上,以相对直接的方法将其翻译成英文。此外,本书中的每首诗歌还标注了汉语拼音。本书中诗歌翻译由中国学者和美国著名汉学家共同完成,以通过向国外受众传播唐宋诗这一文化瑰宝的有益尝试,为中华优秀传统文化走出去提供新的范例。

图书在版编目(CIP)数据

唐宋诗撷英新译/万雪梅,(美)弗雷德里克·特纳(Frederick Turner)编译. --南京:东南大学出版社,2024.12. --ISBN 978-7-5766-1890-7

Ⅰ.I207.22;H315.9

中国国家版本馆 CIP 数据核字第 2024B45E16 号

责任编辑:刘　坚(liu-jian@ seu.edu.cn)	责任校对:张万莹
封面设计:王　玥	责任印制:周荣虎

唐宋诗撷英新译 Tang-Songshi Xieying Xinyi

编　　译	万雪梅　[美国]弗雷德里克·特纳(Frederick Turner)
出版发行	东南大学出版社
出 版 人	白云飞
社　　址	南京市四牌楼2号(邮编:210096　电话:025-83793330)
经　　销	全国各地新华书店
印　　刷	广东虎彩云印刷有限公司
开　　本	787 mm×1 092 mm　1/16
印　　张	20
字　　数	436 千
版　　次	2024 年 12 月第 1 版
印　　次	2024 年 12 月第 1 次印刷
书　　号	ISBN 978-7-5766-1890-7
定　　价	78.00 元

本社图书若有印装质量问题,请直接与营销部调换。电话(传真):025-83791830

江苏大学国家级一流专业"英语"专业建设成果出版编委会

总 主 编：李崇月
编委会成员：张明平　王 蕾
　　　　　　李加军　李 霞

总序
FOREWORD

江苏大学是 2001 年 8 月经教育部批准,由原江苏理工大学、镇江医学院、镇江师范专科学校合并组建的重点综合性大学,是江苏省人民政府和教育部、农业农村部共建高校,也是首批江苏省高水平大学建设高校。

江苏大学英语专业的起源可追溯到 1958 年原镇江师范专科学校开设的英语教育(专科)专业和原江苏工学院 1984 年开设的英语师资班。历经几十年的建设,以英语语种为主体的外国语言文学学科已获得了长足的发展:2003 年获批"外国语言学及应用语言学"二级学科硕士学位点,2018 年获批"外国语言文学"一级学科硕士学位点,2021 年获批"MTI 英语笔译"专业硕士学位点;在近三年(2020、2021、2022)"软科中国最好学科排名"中,江苏大学外国语言文学学科稳居江苏省内高校前六位;得益于外国语言文学学科的有力支撑,近年来,江苏大学英语专业"四级"和"八级"一次性通过率远超全国平均水平;近三年来,本科毕业生考研录取率达 35%;毕业生专业教学满意度在全校 30 多个文管类专业中连续多年位居前列;英语专业特色鲜明,专业建设成绩显著,2021 年获批"国家级一流专业建设点"。

目前,江苏大学英语专业师资力量雄厚。近 30 位教师中,有教授 10 人、副教授 10 人。师资队伍中除了有多位英语语言文学博士外,还有传播学博士、外交学博士和逻辑学博士各 1 人。师资结构有力支撑了英语专业"国际事务与沟通"特色方向的建设。在新文科建设背景下,英语专业教师结合自己的教学及研究专长,紧扣一流专业建设目标,在教师发展研究、课程教材资源开发、教育教学研究等方面取得了一系列成果,现以专著或教材的形式由东南大学出版社出版。

《社会文化理论视角下高校英语教师学习叙事案例研究》(李霞著)基于社会文化理论,对高校英语教师学习经历、学习过程及学习影响因素进行深入系统的探讨,为推动高校英语教师发展提供参考和建议。该研究成果有助于增进学界对高校英语教师学习的了解,激发教师反思自身学习,优化教学实践,实现科学、高效、持久的专业发展,从而进一步推进一流本科英语专业内涵建设及人才培养的高质量发展。

英语文学教材《文学与科学:新文科英语文学》(毛卫强主编)吸纳英语文学跨学科研究方面的成果,在介绍英语文学如何表征、传播甚至参与建构自然科学领域的研究及发现的同时,结合第一手文献资料和具体案例,培养英语专业学生利用自然科学领域相关知识来批判性解读英语文学作品的能力,发展学生的跨学科意识,拓展学生的科学人文素养。

英文教材《翻译简史》(李崇月、张璘主编)从中国学者的视角,以翻译文本类型(如宗教、科技、文学、社科等)和翻译的方向(译入、译出)为经,以历史上有影响的翻译事件和翻译思想为纬,勾勒中外翻译实践和翻译思想的发展脉络,在中外参照对比中突出中国丰富的翻译实践及其对中国文化发展的贡献。教材从总体框架设计、具体史料选择及对翻译事实的解读上都做到了宏观与微观结合、史实与史识相融,囊括了翻译史的主要内容,为我国翻译史的研究和教学提供了新视角。

《世界经典寓言童话故事选读》(叶富莲编著)的选材来自世界经典寓言童话作家的作品,教材从题材、人物、结构、修辞、主题、语言、同类比较等方面对寓言和童话进行了系统化的说明和阐释,各单元包括文本、注解、练习、讨论和写作等内容。本教材一方面可以提高英语专业学生的语言实践能力,另一方面可以引导学生利用相关语言材料进行英语语言教学的模拟实践。

《如何清晰、理性地思维:逻辑与批判性思维能力培养教程》(闫林琼编著)提供了适合中国高校尤其是理工科院校英语专业学生、融合思政要素并且难易度适中的逻辑与批判性思维能力培养教材。教材包括英语专业学生逻辑与批判性思维能力培养的紧迫性,如何提问,如何论证,如何在多种课程教学中培养逻辑与批判性思维能力等内容,有利于弥补英语专业学生逻辑思辨能力的不足。

《中国参与联合国大会人权议程设置的论辩话语研究》(候璐莎著)从中国参与联合国大会人权治理进程的不同阶段出发,考察中国参与联合国大会人权议程设置多边谈判之中影响论辩策略的因素,阐明了中国运用论辩策略来提高谈判说服力、议程设置能力以及国际人权话语权的研究路径。本书有助于培养英语专业学生的批判性思维、国际沟通与应变能力,增强学生用英语合理且有效地表达自己观点的论辩与谈判能力,有助于使其成为具有全球视野、跨文化交际能力的一专多能复合型英语人才。

《镇江文化外宣》(万雪梅编著)体现英语一流专业建设的地方特色,致力于讲好江苏大学所在地镇江的故事。本书提炼镇江文化的精神标识和精髓,从镇江历史、山水、文物、教育、文学、艺术、科技、饮食、对外人文交流等方面展开,呈现可信、可爱、可敬的镇江形象,助推中华文化更好地走向世界。

《唐宋诗撷英新译》(万雪梅、弗雷德里克·特纳编译)选译了李白、杜甫、王维、范仲淹、苏轼等65位唐宋诗人的159首诗作。所选作品皆为唐宋诗中的经典之作,既有哲学意蕴,又有诗学之美。且诗中体现的儒释道情感与精神能够激发起读者和译者的共鸣,对中华优秀传统文化的阐释和传播颇有裨益。

《学术英语能力及其标准建设研究》(钟兰凤编著)收录学术论文13篇,旨在通过对英文学术话语进行分析,兼采用实验法和调查法,探讨学术英语能力标准建设的主要构件:学术英语能力表现研究、学术英语能力培养的路径及影响因素、学术英语能力标准建设的基本路径和设计原则。本研究成果可以直接应用于英语专业必修课"英语学术论文写作"的课程内容改革及教学方法改革。

以上是即将出版的英语专业建设成果，这些成果为江苏大学国家级一流专业"英语"的专业建设作出了极大贡献。我代表江苏大学外国语学院衷心感谢付出辛勤劳动的、从事英语专业教学的同事们，也要感谢教育部外国语言文学类专业教学指导委员会和英语专业教学指导分委员会多位委员长期以来对江苏大学英语专业建设的关心和指导，感谢江苏大学校领导和教务处对英语专业建设的关心和支持，感谢东南大学出版社刘坚老师编辑团队的默默付出。

江苏大学国家级一流专业"英语"专业点建设负责人
李崇月
2023 年 7 月 1 日

前言
PREFACE

唐宋诗不仅是中国文学精髓,也是世界文学文化宝库里的灿烂瑰宝。它高度凝练、富有韵律的语言不仅承载着诗人的思想与情感,而且也承载着中华优秀传统文化,是中华文化文明智慧的结晶。世界上很多国家对它的价值都有所发现,并已有若干外国学者、诗人、翻译家、汉学家等加以译介,使唐宋诗在海外有了比较广泛的传播,产生了持续的影响,展示了良好的中国国家形象。

弗雷德里克·特纳(Frederick Turner, 1943—)就是这些译者中的一位。他祖籍英国,父母皆为人类学家,孩提时期曾随父母在非洲中部度过了数年美好时光。此后,他考入牛津大学,获学士、硕士和博士学位。其间,他与英籍华裔张美琳女士相识,并结为终生伉俪。牛津大学毕业后,赴美国高校任教,兼任过学术杂志主编。他是美国得克萨斯大学达拉斯分校(UTD)人文艺术学院创立教授,集学者、诗人、作家、批评家、翻译家于一身,已出版著作近40部,内容涉及诗歌创作、文学批评理论、比较文学、人类学、心理学、神经系统科学、社会生物学、风景建筑、摄影、行星生物、太空科学、表现理论、教育学、生态恢复、计算物理学、科技历史和哲学、翻译理论、听力学和言语病理学、中世纪和文艺复兴时期文学、博爱理论、媒体研究、建筑和艺术历史等多种跨文化跨学科领域。

初识弗雷德里克·特纳先生,得益于美国得克萨斯大学达拉斯分校顾明栋教授的引荐,感恩他不仅于2011年邀请笔者去该校访学,同时还推荐笔者去听特纳教授所开设的课程。当时,笔者去听的是特纳教授开设的莎士比亚课程,在听课过程中,不时为他在课堂中脱口而出的莎翁作品中的睿智慧话语所叹服。随后，了解到他是UTD传奇式的人物，具有多方面的才能，还开设有诗歌、美学等课程。不仅如此，他还是一位翻译家，获得过翻译方面的奖项，不仅翻译过匈牙利的诗歌，而且还从璀璨瑰丽、浩如星辰的唐宋诗中采撷了159首（其中唐诗134首，宋诗25首），并将之翻译成了英语。毫无疑问，特纳教授不仅喜欢唐宋诗，而且从这些诗歌中发现了那种与他本人相似的哲学视野与美学志趣。正因为如此，他最初花了至少三年的时光，翻译了这些唐宋诗，其间，他曾在其博士生的协助下，来到中国一段时间，就像他作为人类学家的父母去非洲进行田野作业一般，寻访过一些唐宋诗人当年留下的足迹，体悟诗人当年成诗的心境，此后，他从未间断修订完善这些诗。总之，从最初开始翻译到这本书定稿已历时约20年。

正因为如此，笔者在第一次访学回程前，对特纳教授进行了访谈。五年后，又很荣幸地受到了他本人的邀请，再次赴美访学了一年。其间，笔者旁听了他的诗歌和美学等课程，整理、汇编了他翻译的这些唐宋诗，每周都在他固定的对外办公时间，向其求教，与其研讨、对话，对其进行录音访谈等。已发表对其进行的中英文访谈等论文如下：

1.《弗雷德里克·特纳教授访谈录》（英文），《外国语文研究》，2015(1)；

2.《诗歌、诗学与科幻史诗：弗雷德里克·特纳教授访谈录》（英文），《外国文学研究》，2015(6)；

3.《"宇宙诗人"话唐诗》(1—3)，《达拉斯新闻》，2017年10月6日、10月13日、10月20日；

4.《翻译中国唐诗 守护宇宙家园——弗雷德里克·特纳教授访谈录》（英文），《外国语文研究》，2019(4)；

5.《唐诗何为：音乐、生态、救世》，《跨文化对话》（第40辑），乐黛云、[法]李比雄主编，北京：商务印书馆，2019年10月。

弗雷德里克·特纳撷英新译的159首唐宋诗所涉及的作者共65位，其中，唐代诗人49位，宋代诗人16位，这65位唐宋诗人的姓名及其被选译诗歌的具体数目分别为：神秀(1)、慧能(1)、骆宾王(1)、王勃(2)、陈子昂(1)、张九龄(1)、王之涣(2)、孟浩然(2)、王湾(1)、王昌龄(5)、王维(13)、李白(15)、高适(1)、崔颢(3)、杜甫(19)、岑参(1)、张继(1)、刘长卿(1)、金昌绪(1)、韦应物(1)、卢纶(2)、李益(1)、李康成(1)、孟郊(2)、韩翃(1)、王建(2)、张籍(3)、韩愈(1)、刘禹锡(3)、寒山(1)、白居易(5)、李绅(2)、崔护(1)、柳宗元(3)、元稹(1)、贾岛(2)、李贺(6)、朱庆馀(1)、杜牧(5)、李涉(1)、皎然(1)、温庭筠(2)、李商隐(7)、黄巢(1)、韦庄(1)、聂夷中(1)、皮日休(1)、杜荀鹤(2)、秦韬玉(1);林逋(1)、范仲淹(1)、梅尧臣(1)、王安石(4)、程颢(1)、苏轼(4)、李清照(1)、陆游(2)、范成大(2)、杨万里(1)、朱熹(2)、翁卷(1)、叶绍翁(1)、张俞(1)、志南(1)、卢梅坡(1)。

诚如前文所及,特纳教授新译这些唐宋诗并非一蹴而就,同样,笔者编译这些唐宋诗也并非一挥而就,校订、回译、注音、排版等,前后已历经10多年,甚至还会因某处译法联系特纳教授,与其再商榷。在回译、注音及排版初期,笔者所指导的文学院研究生刘乐乐、张媛媛和曾琴,以及我院研究生张蓉蓉都曾为此出力,在此,对她们表示感谢。

一直感动于特纳教授在翻译我国唐宋诗方面所做的努力,这对进一步扩大中国文化的国际影响力,促进中外文明交流互鉴是有积极意义的。因此,笔者一直深感自己有责任去助其完成译作的纸质出版事宜。此前,他自己也曾努力过,但并不顺畅,他已经出版的著作都是国外出版商主动联系他的,而那些出版商中几乎没人懂汉语,更不用说唐宋诗了;于是,为方便读者,他就将自己的译作在国外一家网站上发表了,当然,在他的个人博客上,也能查到,尽管如此,该书如能以纸质版的形式出版,必将惠及全球更多对此有兴趣的读者。

感恩国家对中华优秀传统文化外译的重视,感恩我校我院历届领导的高瞻远瞩与英明引领,感恩我院现任院长李崇月教授等对该书可作为我院英语专业建设成果的认定,感恩江苏大学国家级一流专业"英语"专业建设成果出版编委会的大力资助,感恩东南大学出版社刘坚教授智慧的启迪及严谨的编辑,感谢德国汉学家顾彬先生对特纳教授翻译质量的高度肯定,感恩所有其他我无法在此一一列出姓名但曾经为此书的翻译贡献过力量的中外专家学者。限于笔者水平,书中难免存在问题,特纳教授和笔者都热忱欢迎各位方家的批评指正,不胜区区感激之情。

万雪梅
2023 年 12 月 12 日于京口

INTRODUCTION

The Tang Poets: A Personal View
Frederick Turner

From about the middle of the seventh century to the middle of the eleventh, one of the most remarkable bodies of poetry in the world was composed in China. It is at once achingly fresh and evocative, and classically sophisticated; perhaps the only Western analogy might be the work of the early Greek lyric poets—now mostly lost—and their great Roman followers, Horace and Virgil. The poems from the period in this anthology are for the most part tiny in physical length and astonishingly uniform in structure and meter—but each one is a unique gem of profound water and unplumbed depth.

These poems were selected from the huge body of classical Tang poetry by my collaborator, a Chinese scholar of distinction who chooses, against my wishes but with characteristic Chinese modesty, to remain anonymous. I do not read or speak more than a few Chinese words; during our work on these poems I avoided using other translations, such as those of Witter Bynner, Ezra Pound, and Kenneth Rexroth, though I was familiar with them before. Thus I must acknowledge my great debt to my nameless colleague, for he was, with the exception of some useful comments and advice from the Chinese philologist Baomei Lin and my brilliant editor Xuemei Wan, my only language informant.

These poems roughly overlap the period of the Tang and Song Dynasties, which until its later decline provided an era of peace and prosperity in the heartland of China. For the Han, China's largest ethnic group, the Tang period was the pinnacle of Chinese culture and power, the time when China's "Yang" or brilliant and positive creative energy, was at its strongest, followed by decline. The poems in this anthology do not represent the entire range of genre, form and subject in Tang poetry, but they are a fair sample. This introduction will address only the poems here, and should not be taken as applying to all of Tang poetry, still less to Chinese poetry as a whole. Applying, for the sake of crude historical classification, the traditional Western system of cultural periodization—a practice shared with the Chinese themselves, who write of "Late Tang", "High Tang", "Song Dynasty" etc.—we might describe the poets translated here in this way:

First, the Early Tang poets, such as Meng Haoran, Wang Bo, Wang Zhihuan, and especially Wang Changling. We can compare their purity and sweetness of sensibility to such Western figures as Giotto, Ronsard, Saint-Colombe, and Dowland in their respective cultures and artforms.

Second, the high classicism of Wang Wei, perhaps comparable to Bach or Novalis or Raphael, or—in his perfection of the genre of nature poetry—the great Dutch and English landscape painters.

Third, the mature classicism of Du Fu, perhaps the greatest of all the Tang poets, his exquisite style enriched with psychological depth and controlled passion. Here the objective and subjective are perfectly balanced, as in the work of such Western figures as Shakespeare, Michelangelo, and Mozart.

Fourth, the great mannerist, Li Bai, a giant in the world of subjective artists. Passionate, turbulent, romantic, mystical, fantastical, but with a strange self-deprecating sense of humor, he explores the strange world of Chinese folklore and the darker and wilder passages of the soul—but always with poetic mastery and dignified grace. Perhaps we can compare him with Caravaggio, Beethoven, Milton.

Fifth, the great poet of social protest, Bai Juyi, who sees already the signs of Tang cultural and political decadence, and couches his prophetic and moral message in realistic scenes of ordinary life. Here we must turn to the great Romantic novelists, like Balzac, Tolstoy, and Dickens, or to painters like Millet and Van Gogh, or dramatists like Berthold Brecht, for comparisons.

Sixth, the late Tang and Song period poets: Li He, who like Li Bai explores the Chinese fantasyland, the passions, and the surreal mode, but with a quirkier and gentler charm; Du Mu, with his lovely introspective musings; and the last great flowering in Li Shangyin, lover and philosopher, one of the most exquisite poets of retrospection and delicate feeling, and the Song poets Lu You, Wang Anshi, and Su Shi. Perhaps we might think of such Western "latecomers" as Brahms, Keats, or Caspar David Friedrich. For the purposes of this introduction I shall treat the Song period poets as continuing the stylistic and intellectual tradition of the Tang poets.

The Poet-Scholar's Life

Almost all the recorded Tang poems were composed by poet-scholars who were imperial administrators, or in search of an imperial post, retired or dismissed from such a post, or in voluntary religious retreat from imperial service. The imperial administrator could be as humble as a clerk or as grand as a provincial governor or imperial envoy to the frontier armies; if he remained in the Capital in a position of national responsibility he would have little time or incentive to write, but if his position was that of a minor official he would often be inspired to poetry. More usually he would be sent to the provinces. Wise imperial policy tended to appoint local administrators whose family and childhood home were far away, so as to avoid nepotism and an inter-generational accumulation of local power and wealth that could challenge the distant central government. (To recruit local authorities from distant prefectures was, I believe, the Chinese way of solving the same problem that faced the medieval Christian Church—how to prevent the formation of local dynasties. The Church solved it by enforcing priestly celibacy, so that a priest's or bishop's offspring could have no legal title to the church property. Celibacy was the price a priest paid for his power; exile was the price paid by a mandarin. Louis XIV of France solved it by bringing his nobles to Versailles where he could keep an eye on them). One of the great themes of Tang poetry is exile; family, friends, and the sounds, smells and sights of home became achingly dear, and letters very important. The occasional visit by an old fellow-student would be the occasion of bitter-sweet reminiscence, feastings, late night drinking parties, and sad farewells. Many poems are parting gifts to a friend.

The poetry examination, with its intense period of prior study under professional tutors, was the rite of passage by which a scholar entered imperial service. It is a remarkable reflection that perhaps the longest-lasting regime in the world (setting aside the dynastic struggles of the emperors, and the invasion and swift assimilation of foreign rulers) was the Chinese civil service—and its major qualification was the passing of an examination in poetry! Perhaps this is one reason why China is the only surviving ancient civilization that still uses the same writing system, and the written language of Confucius still remains vivid for modern Chinese. Ernest Fenollosa, like some Chinese scholars, traces the decline after the Tang period to a change of emphasis in the examination system from the composition of original poetry to memorization of Confucian texts—in Chinese terms, a loss of the Yang element in the certification process. For the Tang writer the examinations served as a common ordeal, cementing together in a bond of mutual understanding poets from a hundred corners of China and centuries of Chinese history. A pure and refined poetic vocabulary was hammered out, which was capable of an extraordinary range of delicate nuance, detailed observation, and emotional power.

The ethics and religion of the scholar-poet-administrator were fundamentally Confucian. The prime directive was the perfection of one's own character in virtue and self-restraint through the discipline of letters and the correct performance of pious duty; and the purpose of this purifying discipline was to prepare the scholar to serve the emperor in the just and wise administration of the state. Piety included love for one's family; respect for one's superiors; ritual observance to one's ancestors, to the traditional Chinese deities, and to the emperor; the just and honest conduct of governmental business; and military service as required. But such a life was recognized by most poets to be incomplete without a more meditative and even mystical dimension. Daoist communion with nature and Buddhist retreat for the refreshment of the soul were necessary counterbalances for the worldly cares, vanities, and corruptions of court or command. It was always risky to tell truth to power in China as anywhere else, and such truth-telling was a Confucian duty. In retirement or in dismissal a scholar-poet's religious and ethical life would turn toward Taoist and Buddhist worldviews and practices. He would relinquish ego in search of the secrets of nature and of the soul.

The life of the scholar/administrator supplied many of the major themes of Tang poetry. There is the poem of homesickness: the poet in the wintry western mountains, for instance, hears a familiar melody played on an alien type of flute and misses the southern willows in the spring wind (Wang Zhihuan's "A Song of Liangzhou"). Or looking at the moon over the sea he thinks of distant friends doing the same thing. Then there is the Horatian poem about the rustic wine-party with an old friend and colleague. Or the farewell drunken feast, as the poet in disfavor prepares to depart for a remote post far from the capital (Li Bai's wild and desperate "Bring in the Wine: a Drinking Song"). There is the farewell or parting poem, usually to a friend but sometimes to the beloved wife; and the poem of political exile written to distant friends, yearning for a role in the just reform of government. And there is the war poem, celebrating and mourning the great exploits and sufferings of the frontier; here China's vast Wild West stretches before us, its deserts barred with snow, its distant mountains brooded over by blue clouds. In retirement there is the peace or the grief of an old age that is either serene and wealthy, or lonely and penurious.

The people that wrote these poems more than a thousand years ago were as sophisticated, critical-minded, and well educated as the greatest literary genius of today.

Their sense of humor is fresh and charming, and their social conscience is as sensitive as any today. They possessed a canvas, the vast already-ancient land of China, as varied and rich both historically and geographically, as full of ironic and magnificent perspectives, as that of the West. And they speak to us with both ancient wisdom and delightful directness.

The Content of Tang Poetry

Perhaps the most salient feature of Tang poetry represented here is its attention to nature. If one excepts the romantic poetry of the European nineteenth century, nature poetry is very rare in all human poetic traditions, except as a background for epic or amorous events and as a source of metaphor. But the Chinese were masters of the art of natural description, raising words to the status of paint in the evocation of landscape and weather. Not that Tang poetry is unmetaphorical—the moods and forms of nature always have deeper moral, psychological, religious, and sociopolitical meanings. A nature poem is often a point-to-point allegory, such as Huang Chao's "Ode to the Chrysanthemums" which contrasts the aristocratic peach blossom with the humbler chrysanthemum, in the context of a peasant revolution at the time:

> The west wind rustles in the yard
>   that's thick with your full flower,
> But chill your stamens, cold your scent;
>   no butterflies fly here.

But nature is a powerful value in itself, with a moral presence quite as numinous as in Wordsworth; and the allegory never interferes with the fresh shock of real natural experience. Wang Wei and Du Fu are perhaps the supreme masters of the nature poem, though almost every Tang poet has his own special way of evoking mood and feeling from natural details.

Distinct genres and stock subjects, always renewed by some lovely subtle twist, can be discerned through the centuries of nature verse. The great Chinese waterways inspire the river poems—scholar-administrators traveled mainly by boat, and were well acquainted with riverine scenery and river-port life. There is a whole genre of mountain poetry, with variations: Wang Wei's vast still silences, Li Bai's terrifying precipices, Gao Shi's epic frontier, and the Buddhist mysticism of the Cold Mountain School. There is the seasonal poem, with its precise capture of some special moments—the spring flower festival, the first chill of fall, awakening to snow, the summer storms. There are rain poems and snow poems and mist poems and moon poems and sunset poems and night and morning poems. Each poet would vie respectfully with his predecessors in the topic, and add a unique brush stroke.

Indeed, the metaphor of ink-brush drawing and painting is almost unavoidable. Chinese script, especially when handled by the great scholar poets, who, I am convinced, saw every written character as a rich evocative picture in their heads, is almost inseparable from the visual arts. Often a poem is the text of a painting, the calligraphy subtly matched to the brushwork and stylistic genre of the landscape or the still-life spray of flowers.

Music is scarcely less important to Tang poetry than painting. Very many of the poems are titled "songs", and many were sung as often as recited. One genre of the time was the poem in praise of music, such as Li He's "Upon the Sounds of Li Ping's *Konghou*: Yin", a genre that gives full scope to the Chinese sense of fantasy and an opportunity for the poet to break the strict bonds of brevity and meter that normally discipline his verse. Very often a Tang poetic landscape is haunted by the sound of a flute or the sad notes of the zither-like *zheng*.

The Tang landscape is always inhabited. Even the loneliest and most desolate place has a stretch of guarded frontier wall or a tiny pavilion or the sound of an axe or a bell or a sad flute, or the ghostly presence of past emperors or generals. Just as in the West we find the shepherds and bucolic pastoralists and fishing-folk of Theocritus, Virgil, Sannazaro and Spenser, so in Tang verse there is a cast of arcadian or realistic character types that recurs again and again. The archetypes include the fisherman, the herd-boy with his buffalo, the wise old woodman, the toiling peasant, potter or jade-miner. Again, these thematic figures, though stereotypes, are always given fresh immediacy by some poignant detail.

The nature poetry in this anthology always contains a sense of awe at the sheer vastness of the land of China. The Tang poets loved to climb towers or mountain peaks and survey with a shiver the huge and melancholy scene. Or they would sit in a boat at night while the stars wheeled above them in the black sky, and meditate upon their own insignificance. Then there would come a moment of intense lonely experience, which would find its way into a poem. Likewise, they would survey the ruins of some old imperial palace, recall the extinct passions of that time, and reflect on the transience of all things.

Tang poetry is deeply human and humane. The love poetry in this collection, whose rarity is, I believe, typical of Tang poetry, is always tender and lovely. Du Fu's yearning for his wife in "Moon and Night" is especially moving:

> Dampened with fog, my wife's black fragrant hair
> Falls over jade-cold arms lit by the moon;
> When will we lean upon the airy curtain
> Together in this light, our tears dried? Soon?

Women do not appear much in the masculine world of the scholar-poets in this collection, but when they do they are richly and subtly delineated. Tang poetry has a delightful genre of dramatic monologue in the voice of a lady, full of humor, pathos, psychological insight, and accurate observation—exemplified most famously in Li Bai's "Song of Changgan", translated by Ezra Pound and Ernest Fenollosa as "The River-Merchant's Daughter". The lady's feelings for her lover or husband in such poems again show a huge range, from shy devotion through coquetry and grief-stricken longing to sarcastic insight.

Another perennial topic in Tang poetry is social justice. There seems to be a sense of compassion for the poor in the whole tradition, a compassion that is both sentimental and genuine—Buddhist in its moral spirituality and Confucian in its practical motivation to political and social reform. Bai Juyi is perhaps the master of such themes, though Du Fu and several others have poems on war widows and overtaxed peasants and wretched miners that are as moving.

The poems of social protest almost never attack negligent authorities directly. Sometimes an incident that constitutes in itself a mute indictment of official arrogance, corruption, cowardice, or neglect is simply presented without editorializing. Sometimes an episode of past history that is pointedly relevant to the present is left to stand alone. These stories—of young wives or old mothers deprived of their sons by the draft, of abandoned peasant farms, of lavish court processions and feastings as people die of starvation in distant provinces—are among the most moving of the period. One of the most effective examples of this genre is Bai Juyi's old charcoal-burner spurned aside by the court envoys:

> Though only thin rags hang upon
> His wretched arms and thighs,
> He hopes the winter will be cold
> So charcoal's price will rise.

One foot of snow fell overnight,
He makes an early start;
Down from the hills through rutted ice
He drives the charcoal-cart.

The ox gets tired, the man is starved,
The sun has risen higher,
He rests outside the Southern Gate
Upon the market mire.

Two horsemen lightly canter up;
Who are they? By their dress,
One in yellow, one in plain white,
They're couriers, more or less.

With dispatches in hand, they shout
"Imperial command!"
The old man turns his cart, the ox
Drags the whole burden round.

One cart of charcoal's half a ton;
North to the palace gate
The envoys chivvy him, and now
He must unload the weight.

In grief, he's paid but half a bolt
Of muslin, dyed cheap red,
And but nine feet of low-grade silk
Flung round the ox's head.

  Behind these observations is always a kind of sad and realistic memory of the universal repeated cycle of imperial history: the vital new dynasty that reforms and protects the land, followed by a golden age of wealth and conquest, which yields to luxury and neglect of duty. In its new confidence the dynasty embarks on vainglorious conquests, resulting in stretched supply lines and thus incompetent defense against the perennial invaders, and ends in invasion, rebellion and collapse—with the peasants as always the chief victims. Like other dynasties, the Tang in its later days sent off more and more conscripts to expand the frontier buffer zone or build walls and fortified towns—towns that then had to feed themselves off poor land. The imperial administration taxed the farmers cruelly for these adventures, while depriving them of their young male labor and building sumptuous palaces in the capital, and exiling critical mandarin advisers to remote posts to keep them quiet.

The mood with which the Tang poets responded to official neglect, both of their individual services as pious advisers, and of the nation's welfare as a whole, was the resigned serenity of China's three great religions—Confucianism, Taoism and Buddhism. The Tang poet might meditate on the proverbial Confucian wisdom, like Du Fu in "Beyond the Frontier Pass":

> Who bends a bow should bend one that is strong;
> Who draws an arrow, choose one that is long.
> If you would shoot a man, first shoot his horse;
> To take the enemy, first take their king.
>
> But there must be some end to slaughtering;
> All nations have their own distinct frontiers:
> If we can check aggressive bullying,
> What need for so much killing, harm, and wrong?

Or he might call to mind great historical examples of thankless devotion to Confucian duty, as Du Fu does in "The Shu Prime Minister":

> Where is that noble minister's
>   commemorative shrine?
> Outside the Brocade City, in
>   dark cypress-groves, alone.
> Stone stairways mirror blue-green grass,
>   unkempt in this spring scene;
> A yellow oriole, hid in fronds,
>   sings sweetly, but in vain.

> Three times the nation called on him
> to serve it by his art;
> Two empires the old minister
> guided with all his heart;
>
> He led the troops to victory,
> but died before they won—
> Which wets with tears the garments of
> heroic gentlemen.

Another recourse was to turn one's back on the flattery and corruption of society and enter the strange magical world of Taoist nature mysticism. Nature for the Chinese poet is always liable to surprise him with an epiphanic revelation and a dream vision. Li He is a master of this genre. The most ancient of China's traditions, preserved in old "pagan" myths and fairytales and in memories of early childhood, here rise to the poetic surface as a solace and escape. Perhaps the strangest example is Li Bai's magnificent "Dream Journey on Mount Tianmu: a Farewell Song":

> Fired by this vision, one night I
> dreamed of the land of Yue;
> I'm flying over Mirror Lake,
> where the bright moon holds sway;
> That bright moon casts my shadow on the lake
> And ushers me toward the clear Shan Rill
> Where dwelt the poet-master Xie,
> and his old home is still,
> And over the pure ripples wail
> the apes' cries, sad and shrill.
>
> I don the simple clogs of Master Xie,
> My body climbs the blue cloud ladder way;
> Half up the cliff, look, sunrise on the sea,
> And listen, for the cock crows in the day.
>
> Ten thousand rocks, ten thousand turns,
> The unfixed path winds on;

Tranced by a flower, till sudden dark
    I lean against a stone.

With roars of bears and dragon-screams
    and rumbling waterfalls
I tremble at the forests deep,
    the layered mountain-walls:

Ai! These blue blue clouds
    full of the coming rain!
Ai! These pale pale waters,
    from which the white mist crawls!

Now there's a sudden thunderbolt,
A landslip slumps down from a fault!
There the stone gates of fairyland
Crash open now on either hand,

Reveal a vast and teal-green space,
    a fathomless sky-vault
Where in the sun and moonlight, gold
    and silver towers stand.

Their clothes are glowing rainbows, Ai!
    Their horses, the wild wind;
The gods of cloud, Ai! See their glittering files
    in endless multitudes descend!

The tiger strikes the zither, Ai!
    Those phoenix charioteers!
Ai! See how the Immortal Ones
    their serried ranks extend!

My heart is quaking, Ai!
    My unquiet heart is stirred;
Ah, in this sudden terror
    I wake with a long sigh.

> What's left, alas, is only
> > a pillow and a mat;
> Oh, where is that bright mist now?
> > Where is that rosy cloud?
>
> Thus all the pleasures of the world
> > are transient as a dream,
> Passing forever from the earth
> > as rivers eastward stream.
>
> Farewell, my friend; I do not know
> > the time of my return;
> For now I'll let my white stag graze
> > in these cliffs green with fern—
>
> If called, I'll reascend that peak
> > upon his swift back borne;
> But how shall I with lowered brow
> > and bent neck to the mighty turn,
>
> Where there's no opening of face or heart,
> > in service to their scorn?

Most serene of all religious responses is the Buddhist abandonment of attachment and devotion to the moment of the eternal present. Jiao Ran catches the ethos of the Zen-based Cold Mountain School in his "Hearing a Bell (on Cold Mountain)" (the "ong" rhymes are in the original):

> From the old shrine on Hanshan comes a clang,
> A far bell like the sweet wind's spreading song.
> The Moon-Tree rings with its long lingering,
> The frosty sky is emptied by its gong.
> Long through the night the seeker after Zen
> Lets the mind chill, and still, and hang.

Besides, Tang poets would go on retreats at Buddhist monasteries and seek counsel from the reverend masters.

The Poetic Form of Tang Poetry

All human poetry (with the exception of some free verse experiments in the Westernized countries in the twentieth century) uses a line about three seconds in length when recited, regulated by such devices as syllable-count, stress-count, number and uniformity of metrical feet (established by syllable-length or syllable-stress), tone pattern, grammatical or logical parallelism, alliteration, assonance, consonance, and rhyme. These devices, depending upon the tradition or the poet's choice, can be either voluntary or obligatory—either recognizable ornaments or constitutive features of a given form. For instance, in English a formal sonnet must have fourteen iambic pentameter lines, with one of a small number of rhyme schemes; it may use alliteration, logical and grammatical parallelism, masculine or feminine rhymes, etc.

Chinese Tang period poetry uses a rich palette of rules. It must (with some exceptions, especially in the longer forms) have lines of five or seven syllables. Chinese is of course a tonal language, with four pitched tones (high, rising, falling-and-rising and falling). Certain specific combinations of changing and unchanging tones are required in Tang poetry. There is also to my ear a regular stress pattern of alternating strong and weaker stresses. Lines (again with the exception of the longer forms) are arranged in pairs and quatrains—pairs of pairs. Rhyming is obligatory, though the rhyme pattern can vary and not every line must rhyme. The seven-syllable line will have a caesura after the fourth syllable, like the English "fourteener" (more commonly known as ballad meter) which is divided into eight- and six-syllable parts, with a caesura after the eighth syllable. Chinese poetry also uses a much-prized formal ornament, the couplet, in which a pair of lines echo each other exactly in syntax, while either paralleling or exactly contrasting with each other in logic, and reversing each other in tonal pattern. Even poems that do not contain exact couplets often refer by implication to the couplet in partial parallelisms and significant variations. Assonance, alliteration, etc, are voluntary ornaments, reinforcing the logic or suggesting onomatopoeia. The normal Tang poem has eight or four lines. To my ear—this feature is not often discussed by scholars—the lines are stressed TUM-ta TUM-ta TUM for the five-syllable line, TUM-ta TUM-ta, TUM-ta TUM for the seven-syllable line.

Since Chinese writing is pictographic and ideographic, spoken words being represented not alphabetically but by characters, an additional dimension is added to classical Tang poetry: the semantic interplay among the radicals (the semantic and phonemic visual glyphs out of which a character is composed). Each radical possesses for a Chinese scholar a set of meaningful connotations, which can set up a visual dance through the poem—a dance often heightened by the calligraphy and sometimes echoing the themes of an associated ink-brush painting.

In poetic form as in so many things, such as music, medicine, and painting, the traditional Chinese arts are, it seems to me, an elaboration and brilliant refinement of popular crafts rather than a separate avant-garde intellectual and aesthetic realm. The most recent equivalent in Europe, perhaps, was the music of Bach, where a popular musical tradition was raised to the level of high art without any loss to its capacities for creating direct pleasure and a true sense of community. Though the scholars who created poetry were a distinct class, they often had humble roots, because they were qualified not by birth but by passing an examination; they thus were exposed to the vitality of folk art—the folksong, ballad, fairy tale, etc. Bai Juyi, it is said, would not stop tinkering with his poems until they could be understood by an old cleaning lady. Tang poems were often known by heart among the people and cited proverbially even without awareness of their source, as the Bible still is in the West.

Tang poetry, however, does not seem to have developed the longer forms, the epic, epyllion, or extended dramatic narrative. China had already developed a sophisticated prose, and so the novel or tale forms took over the tasks of more extended storytelling. However, there are some very fine mid-length poems, of upwards of thirty lines, which break out into more extended narrative or spontaneous effusion or meditative discourse. The dithyramb—the longer, irregular, passionate, and sometimes mystical poetry of the inspired Greek bard—may be a useful Western analogy. Li Bai and Du Fu especially show fine examples: Li Bai's "The Perilous Shu Road", "Song of Changgan", and "Dream Journey on Mount Tianmu", and Du Fu's "Song of the War Chariots" and "Thatched Cottage Wrecked by Autumn Gales: a Song" are examples. These longer poems abandon many of the practices of the more formal short poem, mixing five-syllable, seven-syllable, and even longer lines, interspersing exclamations in four or even three syllables, and changing the rhythmic flow. It is as if when a Chinese poet escaped the limits of the quatrain or double quatrain form, a new aesthetic comes into play, one in which precision, delicacy, and perfection is replaced by impressionism, passion, and that roughness that the Italian Renaissance poets called "sprezzatura".

But this is not to imply, either on my part or on that of the Tang poets, that the escape from or breaking of form is necessarily a superior or an inevitable thing. It is only the surrounding presence of a thousand tiny gemlike poems in the tradition that gives meaning and pathos and the force of surprise to the occasional rant or dithyrambic effusion or wandering meditation. And those perfect gems that make up the bulk of the tradition contain in their faceted interiors such blazes of sudden light, color, and emotion as to focus into an ineffable moment the same intensity of feeling that we find, drawn out and elaborated, in the longer poems.

Tang Aesthetic Philosophy

Every great national literature is both unique and at the same time representative of humanity's universal essence. Indeed, what we mean by "great" is perhaps precisely the union of these two characteristics. A literature that was not unique, if one could imagine such a thing, might hardly be worth translating, since its qualities would be available elsewhere; a literature that did not contain the spirit of humanity as a whole would be of local interest only, village gossip or arbitrary cult obsessions. As one might say that all English poetry is in some sense dramatic, and in this uniqueness reveals more clearly than elsewhere the essential dramatic trading that must go on in all good poetry; or that all German poetry is based on a sort of fairy tale in which the novice learns wisdom, and thus tells us something about the guiding function of poetry in general; or that all Hungarian poetry addresses the world of nature and human culture as "thou", and so epitomizes the implicit "ode" element in human poetry—so Tang poetry, when it raises its eyes from the immediate view of the midnight river or mossy tree to the vast and melancholy vision of "ten thousand miles", reflects a hidden theme in all other poetry.

The I Ching system of divination and classification provides a continuous logical progression from the primal unity of Chi energy that is also called the Tao (or "way"), through its first division into Yin and Yang, and successive iterative dividings into binary opposites, into the rich variety of the world. This process resembles the cosmological speculations of modern science. During the Big Bang, physicists tell us, the forces and objects of physics first appeared as a succession of dividings—gravity and the superforce from supergravity, electromagnetism and the electroweak force from the strong nuclear force, the weak nuclear force from electromagnetism, matter and energy from electromagnetism, and so on. The complex dynamical systems of nature attain their full orderly-chaotic structures through an iterative process of folding or bifurcation, a process that is capitalized on by life in its spontaneous protein-folding technique. Likewise, our own fertilized egg becomes a human being through successive cell-divisions, each division creating a more complex three-dimensional geometry, a geometry locally sensed by each cell and guiding its specialization into the organs of the future adult body. The brains of young children grow into neural networks by dendritic branching, and learn natural language by a similar bifurcating and branching system of classification.

The Chinese intuited the basic principles of chaos and complexity theory, which underlie all these processes, long before the West did. Of course the West always had branched systems of classification and taxonomy, as do all human cultures. We do see a similar sequence of creation by iteration and bifurcation in the Hebrew book of Genesis—light divided from darkness, solid from liquid, upper from lower, life from the inanimate, human from non-human, and so on. But these dividings are the work of an intervening divine power that is external to the process; the Chinese saw the divine principle as internal, immanent in the flow of change itself. The creative bifurcations of Hesiod's cosmogony are genealogical, not physical, and so the Greeks did not generalize the principles of growth and reproduction to the inanimate world, and abhorred surds and infinitesimals for the same reason. The Chinese, however, were perfectly at home with inconclusive and undecidable mathematical entities, polycentric dynamical systems and nonlinear causal networks. In Chinese painting one is always being shown the swirls of clouds and water currents, the torsion of mountain-slopes and tree branches, and turbulence of all kinds, as if they were the folds of dancing dragon-bodies pushing through from the visionary world into that of the fleshly eye. In Western painting the basic composition is based on straight lines and Euclidean figures; in Chinese painting, it is as if fractal attractors played the corresponding organizing role. We know now that linear order and straight lines are rare in the universe, and nonlinear dynamical processes are the norm; the Chinese knew this all along, and the strict order of their metrical forms and architecture is a conscious reply and complement to the protean Chi of nature. Just so we find in a scroll painting of a cliffside a tiny pavilion whose straight lines contrast with and complement the surrounding wilderness.

Every Tang poem in this collection celebrates the inner Chi of the world. One might say that for the Tang poet time is not a dimension or a space but a dragonlike energy, an enlivening and animating breath that makes every twig and snowflake shine and transform itself. Chi is not just a dynamic that takes place in time, but the core property of time itself. Chi is both the increase of entropy that constitutes time for thermodynamics, and the self-organizing growth of information that takes place in evolutionary processes. The beauty experience, the shiver of epiphanic delight in every good Tang poem, is a recognition of the promise and power of that energy, the perpetual dawning of the world. Or again, in the terms in which the West rediscovered the old wisdom of the Chinese, our sense of beauty is an intuitive capacity to recognize the strange attractors of nonlinear dynamical processes, especially when those processes are on the brink of self-organizing into a higher integrative level of structure. This moment of emergence is also the point of branching or bifurcation, in which a new kind of entity is precipitated out of some far-from-equilibrium crisis, a turbulence that the old system has encountered in its temporal exploration of the information space. Out of turbulence comes branching; and branching creates new entities. For the Tang poets in this collection, those entities are the germs of poems, which elaborate themselves through pairing and iteration until they are complete. In Du Fu's "Spring Night with Happy Rain" the wild turbulence of wind and rain and flood and cloud resolves in the last two lines into a spring dawn, suddenly full of soaked flowers, and a human city. It is a tiny epitome of the evolution of the universe through the branching of Chi into Yin and Yang, and the continuation of the branching process, drawn by the whispered attractors inherent in the turbulence into the complex forms of flowers and cities:

> A good rain knows the season when it's right,
> In spring, on time, it makes things sprout and grow.
> Follow the wind, sneak out into the night:
> All moist things whisper silently and slow.
>
> Above the wild path, black clouds fill the air,
> The boat-lamp on the flood the only glow;
> At dawn you see wet mounds of crimson where
> The heavy flowers of Chengdu hang down low.

The very form of the classic Tang five-syllable double quatrain exemplifies the mysterious Chi-process of nature. The first line is the Tao of the poem, emerging out of the namelessness of the preceding silence. The second, often forming a couplet with the first, constitutes both its elaboration and its binary contrast, the Yang to its Yin or the Yin to its Yang. The third and fourth echo the relationship between the first and second, but with a further twist. Then the second quatrain takes the theme of the first but in a different key and at a different scale. The universal becomes the particular, the particular is suddenly generalized into a vast universal vision; in either case the correspondence between the form of the macrocosm and the form of the microcosm, their "scaling" or "self-similar" property as fractal geometricians call it, is suddenly brought to mind. But the last line, though it rhymes with some crucial ending earlier in the poem, usually pushes out into an adumbration of some further encounter or development, leaving the reader on the edge of an ineffable discovery of his own. The whole poem is a cube of two lines, suggesting the further implications of its exponential power law. The following, by Wang Wei, is a good example (though Wang Wei likes to vary the classic double quatrain by dividing its sense at the end of the sixth rather than the fourth line, variation upon the theme being the soul of Tang poetry):

The Han River Seen from a High Vantage Point

>The three Xiang forks join at the Chu frontier,
>Through the Jing Gate nine streams pour to the sea;
>The river flows far beyond earth and heaven,
>The mountains seem to be and not to be;
>Cities and realms float by the riverside,
>Great billows roil the void immensity.
>
>Ah yes, Xiangyang has pretty scenery:
>I'll leave to drunk Old Shan the ecstasy!

Our Translation Methods

My co-translator prefers to be called an informant or assistant, but every word of these translations is inspired by meanings that he communicated to me. We worked together for over two years, including a two-week trip to China together in which we visited many of the classic landscapes and cityscapes that the poems describe, and viewed artifacts, calligraphy, and painting of the Tang period.

Our translation work was mostly face-to-face. We met each week for two to three hours, beginning with a recitation by my collaborator in Chinese, in which I noted the cadence, diction, and feeling of the piece. I have picked up some conversational Chinese and recognize many of the words in the Tang classical vocabulary; I know some characters and can discern a number of the radicals. But essentially I am linguistically blind when I come to the language, and my ears and hands must be guided over these poems so that I can visualize their meanings.

My collaborator prepared and brought a trot, which included the Chinese script of the poems, a Pinyin phonetic transcription (including the tonal marks), and a "literal" translation of each word underneath the Pinyin versions. Tang poetry has hardly any syntagmata in the Western sense (words like a, of, the, who, etc) and the logic and argument must be largely inferred from context. One of my biggest challenges was to render into English the rich ambiguities and suggestive alternate readings that result from the syntactical indeterminacy of the original.

We would go through a poem word by word, with explanations by my collaborator of the historical, geographic, biographical, and cultural context and the usage sand connotations of the words. Any issues of rhyme and meter would be thoroughly aired. For instance, in the longer, more irregular poems, I needed to know which variations on the five or seven syllable line were familiar to a Tang audience, and which would come as a deliberate surprise.

I would then prepare an English version, which my collaborator would critique by email or, if the case became complex, at our next meeting. Sometimes I would see a further meaning in the poet's words, using my own poetic intuition of the movement of the poet's mind; sometimes I would have grasped the wrong sense and have to be corrected. My version would attempt to preserve the poem's rhyme scheme, lineation, and cadence, and at least suggest the perfect couplets when they arose. In English, an exact parallel in sound or grammar between two adjacent lines sounds heavy and contrived, because not varied by the Chinese system of tonal contrasts. I usually changed the grammatical sequence while keeping the semantic pairings between the words in each line.

The largest issue that confronted us when we began our work was how to translate the Chinese metrical system into an English equivalent. To translate the seven and five syllable Chinese lines into seven and five syllable English lines was wrong, for several reasons. One reason is that the Chinese lines take about 3.5 and 2.8 seconds respectively to recite, since the Chinese syllable must be drawn out to about twice the length of an English syllable, so as to indicate the important semantic distinctions of tone. An English line of seven syllables would take only about two seconds and sound very short indeed; an English line of five syllables, only about one and a half seconds, would sound like only a fragment of a line. Chinese people can chatter very quickly, but the very character for "poetry" in Chinese contains radicals implying slow and elevated speech.

Another reason is that much of Tang poetic grammar is conveyed, as mentioned earlier, by means of context and word order, whereas English, even though a relatively economical language itself, still requires a host of little prepositions, articles, conjunctions, modal auxiliaries, prefixes, and suffixes to make sense. A pair of Chinese lines, translated word for word, might look like this:

> Mood come oft lone go
> Good thing void self know

—but would need twice the number of syllables to express in English:

> The mood comes often to go out alone;
> There's good only the empty self can know.

(Wang Wei: "The Villa of Mount Zhongnan")

A third reason is that the Tang poetic vocabulary had over centuries of use gathered a huge mass of literary and pictorial connotation and allusion, and conventional metaphoric significance. To suggest these depths requires the full scope of English diction and word-choice.

So I decided to translate one Chinese syllable (or, to say the same thing, one Chinese written character) by two English syllables; thus restoring the actual musical length of the line, giving the opportunity to reveal the logic of the Chinese sentence, and allowing allusion and metaphor theplay they have in the Chinese. When I did this, lo and behold, I ended up with the English ballad meter or fourteener, corresponding to the Chinese seven, and the English pentameter corresponding to the Chinese five. What is lost in this method is the almost picturelike juxtaposition of sememes in the Chinese; but what is gained is the riches of English syntax and affective emphasis, that can bring out the complexity of the Tang poet's mood as polishing brings out the color of a gem. The long English ballad line is usually divided into two, of eight and six syllables; but then again, so is the Chinese seven, into four and three, proving that the Chinese need a caesura after the fourth as we do after the eighth. I have indicated this by indentation, as here, in Gao Shi's melancholy "Ballad of the Yan Country":

> Mountains and rivers desolate
>   stretch to the far frontiers;
> Like windstorms on our flanks there fall

    the horsemen of the Hun;
Dead on the field of battle lie
    half of our halberdiers
Under the tents of generals
    the dancing-girls sing on!

In autumn by the desert fort
    thin grasses withered fall;
At sunset in the lone stronghold
    few troops still keep the wall.
Too often the high-favored ones
    misjudge the enemy,
Their strength spent in the pass, can't hope
    to break the siege at all.

The homesick garrison in arms
    has borne the brunt of war;
Well might the ones they left behind
    weep jade tears in their pain;
Young wives in southern cities are
    breaking their hearts today;
The warriors sent up north of Ji
    turn back their heads in vain.

How might one ever cross once more
    those shimmering frontier plains?
In all this vast and boundless land
    what can avail us here?

Three seasons now, in deathly Chi,
    the clouds are ranged for war,
All night the signal of the watch
    strikes echoes cold and drear.

> They're face to face and sword to sword
>   as blood and snow flow free,
> Did ever yet the noble dead
>   prize fame or eulogy?
>
> Did you not see, sir? —how we fought,
>   how suffered on the battlefield,
> How sorely to this day do we
>   miss the great General Li!

These are the last lines of the poem: note that in the original the penultimate long line breaks the pattern of sevens and expands to eight, preparing a climax in the last line; I have reproduced this effect by making that line a sixteener, divided into eight and eight. I hope that something of the rhythm of the great English border ballad of Chevy Chase comes through here, transmuted into a more courtly and self-conscious key.

目 录 CONTENTS

第一部分　唐　诗

神秀（约 606—706） ……………………………………………………（002）
　佛诗一首 …………………………………………………………………（002）
　One Buddhist Poem ………………………………………………………（002）

慧能（638—713） …………………………………………………………（003）
　佛诗一首 …………………………………………………………………（003）
　One Buddhist Poem ………………………………………………………（003）

骆宾王（约 640—约 684） ………………………………………………（004）
　咏鹅 ………………………………………………………………………（004）
　Geese ………………………………………………………………………（004）

王勃（约 650—约 676） …………………………………………………（005）
　送杜少府之任蜀州 ………………………………………………………（005）
　Farewell to Junior Prefect Du, on His Departure to Take Office in Shuzhou ……
　………………………………………………………………………………（006）
　山中 ………………………………………………………………………（007）
　In the Mountains …………………………………………………………（007）

陈子昂（661—702） ………………………………………………………（008）
　登幽州台歌 ………………………………………………………………（008）
　Climbing the Tower of Youzhou …………………………………………（008）

张九龄（678—740） ………………………………………………………（009）
　望月怀远 …………………………………………………………………（009）
　A Full Moon: Missing Distant Family Members ………………………（010）

王之涣（688—742） .... (011)
    凉州词 .... (011)
    A Song of Liangzhou .... (011)
    登鹳雀楼 .... (012)
    Climbing the Tower of Guanque .... (012)

孟浩然（689—740） .... (013)
    春晓 .... (013)
    Spring Morning .... (013)
    过故人庄 .... (014)
    I Stop by at an Old Friend's Farmhouse .... (015)

王湾（693—751） .... (016)
    次北固山下 .... (016)
    Lodging Beneath Mount Beigu .... (017)

王昌龄（698—756） .... (018)
    芙蓉楼送辛渐 .... (018)
    Farewell to My Guest Xin Jian at the Lotus Pagoda ...... (018)
    闺怨 .... (019)
    Sorrow in a Lady's Chamber .... (019)
    出塞 .... (020)
    Beyond the Great Wall .... (020)
    从军行·其四 .... (021)
    Joining the Army (No. 4) .... (021)
    从军行·其五 .... (022)
    Joining the Army (No. 5) .... (022)

王维（701—761） .... (023)
    使至塞上 .... (023)
    Embassy to the Frontier Pass .... (024)
    鹿柴 .... (025)
    Deer Park .... (025)
    相思 .... (026)
    Longing Memories .... (026)
    九月九日忆山东兄弟 .... (027)

On the Double Ninth Festival, I Remember My Brothers East of Mount Hua ……
……………………………………………………………………………… (027)
竹里馆 ……………………………………………………………… (028)
The Guest House in the Bamboos …………………………… (028)
山居秋暝 …………………………………………………………… (029)
Autumn Evening at Home in the Mountains ……………… (030)
终南山 ……………………………………………………………… (031)
The Zhongnan Mountain ……………………………………… (032)
汉江临眺 …………………………………………………………… (033)
The Han River Seen from a High Vantage Point ………… (034)
渭川田家 …………………………………………………………… (035)
Peasants by the River Wei …………………………………… (036)
渭城曲 ……………………………………………………………… (037)
Song of Weicheng City ……………………………………… (037)
鸟鸣涧 ……………………………………………………………… (038)
Birds Singing in the Ravine ………………………………… (038)
终南别业 …………………………………………………………… (039)
The Villa of Mount Zhongnan ……………………………… (040)
酬张少府 …………………………………………………………… (041)
In Return for a Poem from Deputy Prefect Zhang ……… (042)

李白（701—762） …………………………………………………… (043)
赠汪伦 ……………………………………………………………… (043)
For Wang Lun ………………………………………………… (043)
静夜思 ……………………………………………………………… (044)
Thoughts in a Silent Night …………………………………… (044)
渡荆门送别 ………………………………………………………… (045)
Farewell, Upon Passing Mount Jingmen …………………… (046)
登金陵凤凰台 ……………………………………………………… (047)
Ascending the Phoenix Tower of Jinling …………………… (048)
蜀道难 ……………………………………………………………… (049)
The Perilous Shu Road ……………………………………… (050)
早发白帝城 ………………………………………………………… (057)

Early Start from White King City …………………………………………（057）
　　丁都护歌 ……………………………………………………………………（058）
　　Song of Frontier Commander Ding …………………………………………（059）
　　长干行 ………………………………………………………………………（060）
　　Song of Changgan ……………………………………………………………（061）
　　将进酒 ………………………………………………………………………（066）
　　Bring in the Wine: a Drinking Song …………………………………………（067）
　　月下独酌·其一 ……………………………………………………………（070）
　　Drinking Alone Under the Moon (No. 1) ……………………………………（071）
　　行路难·其一 ………………………………………………………………（072）
　　In Difficulty (No. 1) …………………………………………………………（073）
　　宣州谢朓楼饯别校书叔云 …………………………………………………（074）
　　The Poet's Farewell Dinner for His Uncle, Secretary Li Yun, in the Xie Tiao Tower
　　of Xuanzhou …………………………………………………………………（075）
　　长相思·其一 ………………………………………………………………（076）
　　Long Have I Longed for You (No. 1) …………………………………………（077）
　　塞下曲·其一 ………………………………………………………………（078）
　　Songs of the Frontier Fortress (No. 1) ………………………………………（079）
　　梦游天姥吟留别 ……………………………………………………………（080）
　　Dream Journey on Mount Tianmu: a Farewell Song …………………………（081）
高适（**702—765**） ………………………………………………………（088）
　　别董大 ………………………………………………………………………（088）
　　Farewell to Mr. Dong, the Eldest Son of the Family …………………………（088）
崔颢（**704？—754**） ……………………………………………………（089）
　　黄鹤楼 ………………………………………………………………………（089）
　　Yellow Crane Tower …………………………………………………………（090）
　　长干行·其一 ………………………………………………………………（091）
　　Songs of Changgan (No. 1) …………………………………………………（091）
　　长干行·其二 ………………………………………………………………（092）
　　Songs of Changgan (No. 2) …………………………………………………（092）
杜甫（**712—770**） ………………………………………………………（093）
　　绝句四首·其三 ……………………………………………………………（093）

Four Quatrains (No. 3)	(093)
望岳	(094)
Distant View of the Great Mountain	(095)
春夜喜雨	(096)
Spring Night with Happy Rain	(097)
春望	(098)
Spring: Gazing into the Distance	(099)
前出塞九首·其六	(100)
Beyond the Frontier Pass (No. 6)	(101)
蜀相	(102)
The Shu Prime Minister	(103)
兵车行	(104)
Song of the War Chariots	(105)
对雪	(110)
Facing the Snow	(111)
茅屋为秋风所破歌	(112)
Thatched Cottage Wrecked by Autumn Gales: a Song	(113)
赠花卿	(116)
For My Dear Friend Hua	(116)
登岳阳楼	(117)
Climbing the Tower of Yueyang	(118)
旅夜书怀	(119)
At Night Far From Home He Unburdens His Heart	(120)
月夜	(121)
Moon and Night	(122)
石壕吏	(123)
The Sergeant of Stone Moat Village	(124)
登高	(127)
Ascending a High Place	(128)
咏怀古迹五首·其三	(129)
Lament in Ancient Places (No. 3)	(130)
客至	(131)

My Guest Arrives …………………………………………… (132)
　　闻官军收河南河北 ………………………………………… (133)
　　On Hearing that Imperial Troops Have Recaptured Henan and Hebei …… (134)
　　江汉 ………………………………………………………… (135)
　　On the River ………………………………………………… (136)

岑参(715—770) ……………………………………………… (137)
　　白雪歌送武判官归京 ……………………………………… (137)
　　Song of the White Snow: Farewell to Secretary Wu on His Return to the Capital …
　　…………………………………………………………… (138)

张继(约715—约779) ………………………………………… (141)
　　枫桥夜泊 …………………………………………………… (141)
　　Nocturne: Lying at Anchor by the Maple Bridge ………… (141)

刘长卿(约726—789或790) ………………………………… (142)
　　逢雪宿芙蓉山主人 ………………………………………… (142)
　　Staying on a Night of Wind and Snow with the Host of Hibiscus Mountain ……
　　…………………………………………………………… (142)

金昌绪(不详) ………………………………………………… (143)
　　春怨 ………………………………………………………… (143)
　　Spring Vexation …………………………………………… (143)

韦应物(约737—791) ………………………………………… (144)
　　滁州西涧 …………………………………………………… (144)
　　The West Ravine of Chuzhou ……………………………… (144)

卢纶(739—799) ……………………………………………… (145)
　　和张仆射塞下曲·其二 …………………………………… (145)
　　In Reply to Supervisor Zhang Songs of the Frontier(No. 2) …… (145)
　　和张仆射塞下曲·其三 …………………………………… (146)
　　In Reply to Supervisor Zhang Songs of the Frontier(No. 3) …… (146)

李益(746—829) ……………………………………………… (147)
　　江南曲 ……………………………………………………… (147)
　　Song to a Melody of the South of Yangtze River ………… (147)

李康成(不详) ………………………………………………… (148)
　　采莲曲 ……………………………………………………… (148)

  Plucking Lotuses: A Song ……………………………………………… (149)

孟郊(751—814) …………………………………………………………… (150)
  洛桥晚望 …………………………………………………………… (150)
  Distant View of the Luo Bridge ………………………………… (150)
  游子吟 ………………………………………………………………… (151)
  Song of a Wayfarer ………………………………………………… (152)

韩翃(不详) ……………………………………………………………… (153)
  寒食 …………………………………………………………………… (153)
  The Cold Food Festival …………………………………………… (153)

王建(765—830) …………………………………………………………… (154)
  雨过山村 …………………………………………………………… (154)
  I Pass Through a Mountain Village in the Rain ……………… (154)
  望夫石 ………………………………………………………………… (155)
  A Stone, She Gazes After Her Husband ……………………… (155)

张籍(约767—约830) ……………………………………………………… (156)
  凉州词·其一 ……………………………………………………… (156)
  Song of Liang Zhou (No. 1) ……………………………………… (156)
  征妇怨 ………………………………………………………………… (157)
  Lament of the Conscript's Wife ………………………………… (158)
  节妇吟·寄东平李司空师道 …………………………………… (159)
  Song of the Loyal Wife …………………………………………… (160)

韩愈(768—824) …………………………………………………………… (161)
  听颖师弹琴 ………………………………………………………… (161)
  On Hearing Reverend Master Ying Play the *Qin* …………… (162)

刘禹锡(772—842) ………………………………………………………… (165)
  乌衣巷 ………………………………………………………………… (165)
  The Lane of the Black Robes …………………………………… (165)
  西塞山怀古 ………………………………………………………… (166)
  Xisai Mountain: A Meditation on the Past …………………… (167)
  竹枝词二首·其一 ……………………………………………… (168)
  Bamboo Frond Song (No. 1) ……………………………………… (168)

寒山(不详) ……………………………………………………………… (169)

无题 ………………………………………………………………… (169)
　　Untitled ………………………………………………………………… (170)
白居易(772—846) ………………………………………………………………… (171)
　　夜雪 ………………………………………………………………… (171)
　　Night Snow ………………………………………………………………… (171)
　　赋得古原草送别 ………………………………………………………………… (172)
　　On Parting from a Friend on the Ancient Grasslands ……………………… (173)
　　钱塘湖春行 ………………………………………………………………… (174)
　　Spring Outing at Qiantang Lake ……………………………………………… (175)
　　买花 ………………………………………………………………… (176)
　　Buying Flowers ………………………………………………………………… (177)
　　卖炭翁 ………………………………………………………………… (180)
　　The Old Charcoal-Seller ……………………………………………………… (181)
李绅(772—846) ………………………………………………………………… (184)
　　悯农二首·其一 ………………………………………………………………… (184)
　　A Pair of Ancient Ballads Sympathy for the Peasants(No.1) ……………… (184)
　　悯农二首·其二 ………………………………………………………………… (185)
　　A Pair of Ancient Ballads Sympathy for the Peasants(No.2) ……………… (185)
崔护(772—846) ………………………………………………………………… (186)
　　题都城南庄 ………………………………………………………………… (186)
　　Inscribed on a Door in the South Neighborhood of the Capital …………… (186)
柳宗元(773—819) ………………………………………………………………… (187)
　　登柳州城楼寄漳汀封连四州 ……………………………………………… (187)
　　Ascending the Barbican of Liuzhou for the Four Governors of Zhangzhou, Tingzhou, Fengzhou, and Lianzhou ………………………………………………… (188)
　　渔翁 ………………………………………………………………… (189)
　　The Old Fisherman ……………………………………………………………… (190)
　　江雪 ………………………………………………………………… (191)
　　Snow River ………………………………………………………………… (191)
元稹(779—831) ………………………………………………………………… (192)
　　行宫 ………………………………………………………………… (192)
　　The Country Palace ……………………………………………………………… (192)

贾岛（779—843） ……………………………………………………（193）
　　剑客 ………………………………………………………………（193）
　　The Gentle Swordsman …………………………………………（193）
　　寻隐者不遇 ………………………………………………………（194）
　　I Visit the Hermit, but He Is Not There ………………………（194）

李贺（790—816） ……………………………………………………（195）
　　南园·其一 ………………………………………………………（195）
　　Southern Garden (No. 1) …………………………………………（195）
　　金铜仙人辞汉歌 …………………………………………………（196）
　　The Copper-Gold God's Farewell to the Realm of Han: Song ……（197）
　　雁门太守行 ………………………………………………………（198）
　　Song: the Commander of Wild Goose Gate ……………………（199）
　　老夫采玉歌 ………………………………………………………（200）
　　Song of the Old Jade Miner ………………………………………（201）
　　李凭箜篌引 ………………………………………………………（202）
　　Upon the Sounds of Li Ping's *Konghou*: Yin …………………（203）
　　梦天 ………………………………………………………………（206）
　　Dream Sky …………………………………………………………（207）

朱庆馀（797—？） …………………………………………………（208）
　　近试上张水部 ……………………………………………………（208）
　　Presented to Mr. Zhang of the Water Ministry on the Eve of My Examination
　　………………………………………………………………………（208）

杜牧（803—852） ……………………………………………………（209）
　　泊秦淮 ……………………………………………………………（209）
　　Moored by the Qinhuai River ……………………………………（209）
　　江南春 ……………………………………………………………（210）
　　Spring in the South of Yangtze River ……………………………（210）
　　山行 ………………………………………………………………（211）
　　Mountain Journey …………………………………………………（211）
　　赠别·其二 ………………………………………………………（212）
　　Parting Gift (No. 2) ………………………………………………（212）
　　秋夕 ………………………………………………………………（213）

Autumn Night ………………………………………………… (213)
李涉(不详) ……………………………………………………… (214)
　　　牧童词 …………………………………………………………… (214)
　　　Song of the Boy Cowherd ………………………………………… (215)
皎然(不详) ……………………………………………………… (216)
　　　闻钟 ……………………………………………………………… (216)
　　　Hearing a Bell (on Cold Mountain) ……………………………… (217)
温庭筠(约812—866) …………………………………………… (218)
　　　商山早行 ………………………………………………………… (218)
　　　Early Departure on Mount Shang ………………………………… (219)
　　　赠少年 …………………………………………………………… (220)
　　　For a Young Man ………………………………………………… (220)
李商隐(约813—约858) ………………………………………… (221)
　　　嫦娥 ……………………………………………………………… (221)
　　　The Moon Goddess Chang'e ……………………………………… (221)
　　　无题 ……………………………………………………………… (222)
　　　Untitled …………………………………………………………… (223)
　　　锦瑟 ……………………………………………………………… (224)
　　　The Inlaid Zither ………………………………………………… (225)
　　　隋宫 ……………………………………………………………… (226)
　　　The Palace of the Sui Emperor …………………………………… (227)
　　　夜雨寄北 ………………………………………………………… (228)
　　　A Letter to the North Written on a Rainy Night ………………… (228)
　　　乐游原 …………………………………………………………… (229)
　　　Leyou Plateau …………………………………………………… (229)
　　　晚晴 ……………………………………………………………… (230)
　　　A Fine Evening …………………………………………………… (231)
黄巢(820—884) ………………………………………………… (232)
　　　题菊花 …………………………………………………………… (232)
　　　Ode to the Chrysanthemums …………………………………… (232)
韦庄(约836—910) ……………………………………………… (233)
　　　台城 ……………………………………………………………… (233)

Tai City ……………………………………………………………（233）
聂夷中（837—884）……………………………………………（234）
　　咏田家 ……………………………………………………………（234）
　　Lament of the Peasant Family …………………………………（235）
皮日休（约838—约883）………………………………………（236）
　　汴河怀古·其二 …………………………………………………（236）
　　The Bian River Reach of the Grand Canal：A Meditation（No. 2）…………（236）
杜荀鹤（846—904）……………………………………………（237）
　　山中寡妇 …………………………………………………………（237）
　　The Widow in the Mountains ……………………………………（238）
　　送人游吴 …………………………………………………………（239）
　　Farewell to a Friend on His Departure for the Land of Wu ………（240）
秦韬玉（不详）…………………………………………………（241）
　　贫女 ………………………………………………………………（241）
　　Poor Girl …………………………………………………………（242）

第二部分　宋　诗

林逋（967—1028）………………………………………………（244）
　　山园小梅二首·其一 ……………………………………………（244）
　　Plum Blossoms in the Mountain Garden（No. 1）………………（245）
范仲淹（989—1052）……………………………………………（246）
　　江上渔者 …………………………………………………………（246）
　　Fisherman upon the River ………………………………………（246）
梅尧臣（1002—1060）…………………………………………（247）
　　陶者 ………………………………………………………………（247）
　　The Potter's Song ………………………………………………（247）
王安石（1021—1086）…………………………………………（248）
　　登飞来峰 …………………………………………………………（248）
　　Ascending Feilai Peak ……………………………………………（248）
　　梅花 ………………………………………………………………（249）
　　Wintersweet ………………………………………………………（249）

泊船瓜洲 …………………………………………………………（250）
　　Mooring at Guazhou …………………………………………（250）
　　元日 ……………………………………………………………（251）
　　Lunar New Year's Day ………………………………………（251）
程颢（1032—1085） ………………………………………………（252）
　　春日偶成 ………………………………………………………（252）
　　Impromptu Lines on a Spring Day …………………………（252）
苏轼（1037—1101） ………………………………………………（253）
　　题西林壁 ………………………………………………………（253）
　　Inscribed on a Temple Wall …………………………………（253）
　　惠崇春江晚景 …………………………………………………（254）
　　Hui Chong's River Scenes on a Spring Evening …………（254）
　　惠州一绝 ………………………………………………………（255）
　　Glorious Huizhou ……………………………………………（255）
　　饮湖上初晴后雨 ………………………………………………（256）
　　Drinking on the Lake: First Shine, Then Rain ……………（256）
李清照（1084—1155） ……………………………………………（257）
　　夏日绝句 ………………………………………………………（257）
　　Quatrain for a Summer Day …………………………………（257）
陆游（1125—1210） ………………………………………………（258）
　　冬夜读书示子聿 ………………………………………………（258）
　　Teaching Ziyu to Read on a Winter's Night ………………（258）
　　游山西村 ………………………………………………………（259）
　　Visiting the Village to the West of Sanshan Township ……（260）
范成大（1126—1193） ……………………………………………（261）
　　四时田园杂兴·其二十五 ……………………………………（261）
　　Garden Poems of the Four Seasons（No. 25）………………（261）
　　四时田园杂兴·其三十一 ……………………………………（262）
　　Garden Poems of the Four Seasons（No. 31）………………（262）
杨万里（1127—1206） ……………………………………………（263）
　　小池 ……………………………………………………………（263）
　　A Little Pond …………………………………………………（263）

朱熹（1130—1200） ·· （264）
    观书有感·其一 ··· （264）
    Reflections on Reading Books (No. 1) ························· （264）
    偶成 ··· （265）
    Composed by Accident ··· （265）

翁卷（1163—1245） ·· （266）
    乡村四月 ·· （266）
    The Village in April ·· （266）

叶绍翁（1194—1269） ··· （267）
    游园不值 ·· （267）
    Visiting a Garden but Denied Entrance ························ （267）

张俞（不详） ··· （268）
    蚕妇 ··· （268）
    The Silkworm Girl ·· （268）

志南（不详） ··· （269）
    绝句 ··· （269）
    A Quatrain ·· （269）

卢梅坡（不详） ·· （270）
    雪梅·其二 ·· （270）
    Snow and Plum Blossom (No. 2) ································ （270）

第一部分

唐　诗

神秀（约606—706）

佛诗一首

身是菩提树，

心如明镜台，

时时勤拂拭，

莫使有尘埃。

Shenxiu (c 606—706)

One Buddhist Poem

The body is a holy bodhi tree,

The heart a mirror polished to a glow;

So it reflects the truth, clean it each day,

Lest dust be drawn to grime its purity.

慧能 (638—713)

佛诗一首

菩提本无树，

明镜亦非台，

本来无一物，

何处惹尘埃。

Huineng (638—713)

One Buddhist Poem

The bodhi is no body and no tree,

There's no bright mirror to corrode or rust;

At first no thing at all had come to be,

So what is there to draw the grime and dust?

骆宾王 (约640—约684)

咏鹅

鹅，鹅，鹅，
曲项向天歌。
白毛浮绿水，
红掌拨清波。

Luo Binwang (c 640—c 684)

Geese

Honk, honk, honk!

Crook-necked, the geese raise clamor to the sky,

White feathers floating in the water's green,

Red paddles rowing in the clear bright wave.

王　勃（约650—约676）

送杜少府之任蜀州

城阙辅三秦，
风烟望五津。
与君离别意，
同是宦游人。
海内存知己，
天涯若比邻。
无为在歧路，
儿女共沾巾。

Wangbo (c 650—c 676)

Farewell to Junior Prefect Du, on His Departure to Take Office in Shuzhou

The land of Three Qin guards upon Chang'an;

I gaze toward five ferries; smoke and wind.

Sadly I say goodbye to you, my friend,

Both of us official travelling men.

Soul mates we are, between the four great seas,

Neighbors, though at the world's remotest end;

Let us not linger at the road's fork, then,

Like tender children, wetting handkerchieves.

王勃（约650—约676）

山中

长江悲已滞，

万里念将归。

况属高风晚，

山山黄叶飞。

Wangbo (c 650—c 676)

In the Mountains

Why must the Yangtze flow so sluggishly?

Ten thousand *li* I yearn for my return.

And it's so late, the autumn wind blows high

And through the hills, the hills, the gold leaves fly.

chén zǐ áng
陈子昂(661—702)

dēng yōu zhōu tái gē
登幽州台歌

qián bù jiàn gǔ rén
前 不 见 古 人,

hòu bù jiàn lái zhě
后 不 见 来 者。

niàn tiān dì zhī yōu yōu
念 天 地 之 悠 悠,

dú chuàng rán ér tì xià
独 怆 然 而 涕 下!

Chen Ziang (661—702)

Climbing the Tower of Youzhou

I cannot see all those who went before,

All those who are to come I cannot see.

Then in my loneliness and grief the tears roll down,

For heaven and earth appear so vast, so vast to me.

张九龄（678—740）

望月怀远

海上生明月，
天涯共此时。
情人怨遥夜，
竟夕起相思。
灭烛怜光满，
披衣觉露滋。
不堪盈手赠，
还寝梦佳期。

Zhang Jiuling (678—740)

A Full Moon: Missing Distant Family Members

Out of the ocean grows the brilliant moon,

From furthest shores family members share this moment too;

Grieving, they wish this long night over soon,

Awake, remembering, the whole night through.

I douse the wick, in love with the moonlight;

Throw on some clothes, moist with the falling dew.

Couldn't I give you armfuls of bright night!

But I go back to sleep and dreams of you.

王之涣(688—742)

凉州词

黄河远上白云间，
一片孤城万仞山。
羌笛何须怨杨柳，
春风不度玉门关。

Wang Zhihuan (688—742)

A Song of Liangzhou

The Yellow River climbs away
　　to far white clouds and sky;
A lonely outpost fortress lies
　　in mountains ten miles high.
Qiang flute, why must you take to heart
　　the "Willow" song, alas?
You know the spring wind never blows
　　across the Yumen Pass.

王之涣 (688—742)

登鹳雀楼

白日依山尽，
黄河入海流。
欲穷千里目，
更上一层楼。

Wang Zhihuan (688—742)

Climbing the Tower of Guanque

The white sun nears the mountain, shines no more;
The Yellow River flows into the sea;
If you would stretch your eye one thousand *li*,
You must climb one more storey of the tower.

mèng hào rán
孟 浩 然（689—740）

chūn xiǎo
春　晓

chūn mián bù jué xiǎo,
春　眠　不　觉　晓，

chù chù wén tí niǎo.
处　处　闻　啼　鸟。

yè lái fēng yǔ shēng,
夜　来　风　雨　声，

huā luò zhī duō shǎo.
花　落　知　多　少。

Meng Haoran (689—740)

Spring Morning

My spring sleep did not feel the first dawn air,

But now I hear the birds sing everywhere.

Throughout the night the sound of wind and rain—

Who knows how many flowers fell, out there!

孟浩然(mèng hào rán)(689—740)

过故人庄 (guò gù rén zhuāng)

故人具鸡黍,
(gù rén jù jī shǔ)

邀我至田家。
(yāo wǒ zhì tián jiā)

绿树村边合,
(lù shù cūn biān hé)

青山郭外斜。
(qīng shān guō wài xié)

开轩面场圃,
(kāi xuān miàn cháng pǔ)

把酒话桑麻。
(bǎ jiǔ huà sāng má)

待到重阳日,
(dài dào chóng yáng rì)

还来就菊花。
(huán lái jiù jú huā)

Meng Haoran (689—740)

I Stop by at an Old Friend's Farmhouse

My old friend cooks a chicken millet stew,

He's asked me to his farm to share a meal.

A clump of green trees lines the village side,

Blue mountains slant above the city wall.

Flowers and a threshing floor outside the window,

We drink, talk hemp and mulberries and all;

Wait till the Chongyang Festival: I'll come

In time for the chrysanthemums in fall.

王 wáng 湾 wān (693—751)

次北固山下
cì běi gù shān xià

客路青山外，
kè lù qīng shān wài

行舟绿水前。
xíng zhōu lǜ shuǐ qián

潮平两岸阔，
cháo píng liǎng àn kuò

风正一帆悬。
fēng zhèng yī fān xuán

海日生残夜，
hǎi rì shēng cán yè

江春入旧年。
jiāng chūn rù jiù nián

乡书何处达？
xiāng shū hé chù dá

归雁洛阳边。
guī yàn luò yáng biān

Wangwan (693—751)

Lodging Beneath Mount Beigu

The traveler's way leads past the verdant peaks,

The boat glides swifter than the teal-green flow;

The flood has widened level with the banks,

My one sail hangs, the breeze blows calm and slow.

The far sea's sun grows from the dregs of night;

The river's spring invades the old year. So,

If I wrote letters home, where would they go?

Back with the wild geese to Luoyang far below.

王昌龄（698—756）

芙蓉楼送辛渐

寒雨连江夜入吴，
平明送客楚山孤。
洛阳亲友如相问，
一片冰心在玉壶。

Wang Changling (698—756)

Farewell to My Guest Xin Jian at the Lotus Pagoda

Cold rain and river drift and drift
　　through Wu-land's midnight shade;

At dawn we'll part; in Chu's lone hills
　　your journey must be made.

In Luoyang tell my kith and kin
　　if they ask after me,

That I am but a crystal heart
　　within an urn of jade.

王昌龄（698—756）

闺怨

闺中少妇不知愁，

春日凝妆上翠楼。

忽见陌头杨柳色，

悔教夫婿觅封侯。

Wang Changling (698—756)

Sorrow in a Lady's Chamber

In her bedchamber the young wife
    has never known despair;

But dressed and painted, this spring day,
    climbing her emerald stair,

She sees along the country lane
    the weeping willows' green,

Grieves that she sent her lord away
    to seek high honors there.

wáng chāng líng
王昌龄 (698—756)

chū sài
出 塞

qín shí míng yuè hàn shí guān
秦 时 明 月 汉 时 关,

wàn lǐ cháng zhēng rén wèi huán
万 里 长 征 人 未 还。

dàn shǐ lóng chéng fēi jiàng zài
但 使 龙 城 飞 将 在,

bù jiào hú mǎ dù yīn shān
不 教 胡 马 度 阴 山。

Wang Changling (698—756)

Beyond the Great Wall

As in Qin times the moon, the pass,
   so in the time of Han;

Young soldiers march ten thousand *li*,
   and do not yet return.

Were the famed "Flying General"
   of Dragon City here,

We'd never let Hun cavalry
   across Mount Yin's frontier!

王昌龄(698—756)

从军行·其四

青海长云暗雪山，

孤城遥望玉门关。

黄沙百战穿金甲，

不破楼兰终不还。

Wang Changling（698—756）

Joining the Army（No.4）

Long cloud racks over Lake Qinghai
shade mountains white with snow;

The lonely fort faces the distant
Jade-Gate pass.

A hundred battles in the sands
wear out the mail and chain;

If we do not defeat Loulan,
may none return again!

王昌龄 (698—756)

从军行·其五

大漠风尘日色昏,
红旗半卷出辕门。
前军夜战洮河北,
已报生擒吐谷浑。

Wang Changling (698—756)

Joining the Army (No. 5)

The desert sandstorm turns the sun
 a dusky yellow-gray;

The red war-banner's furled as they
 pass through the fort's gateway.

Alone the vanguard fights tonight
 north of the River Tao;

Reports come in that Tuyuhun,
 the chief, is captured now.

王维 (701—761)
使至塞上

单车欲问边，
属国过居延。
征蓬出汉塞，
归雁入胡天。
大漠孤烟直，
长河落日圆。
萧关逢候骑，
都护在燕然。

Wangwei (701—761)

Embassy to the Frontier Pass

To visit the frontier I drove alone;

As special envoy I had passed Juyan.

Tumbleweed blown beyond the lands of Han,

The wild geese seeking foreign skies again.

In the great desert one tall line of smoke,

On the long river, round, the setting sun:

A mounted scout comes to me in Xiao Guan,

Says the commander is on Mount Yanran.

王维 (701—761)

鹿柴

空山不见人，
但闻人语响。
返景入深林，
复照青苔上。

Wangwei (701—761)

Deer Park

The mountain's empty of all human sign

But for a voice that rings out far below.

The backlit forest casts deep shafts that shine

Upon the moss, give back a bright green glow.

王维 (701—761)

相思

红豆生南国，
春来发几枝？
愿君多采撷，
此物最相思。

Wangwei (701—761)

Longing Memories

The red bean grows down in the southern lands,

In spring, it sprouts how many filigrees?

Please gather, sir, armfuls of these sweet shoots:

Such things arouse the richest memories.

王维 (701—761)

九月九日忆山东兄弟

独在异乡为异客,

每逢佳节倍思亲。

遥知兄弟登高处,

遍插茱萸少一人。

Wangwei (701—761)

On the Double Ninth Festival, I Remember My Brothers East of Mount Hua

A foreign guest, and all alone, stranger in a strange land,

I yearn, each happy holiday, twice for my own dear kind.

I know my distant brothers on whatever height they've climbed

Have set one extra cornel for the one they left behind.

王维 (701—761)

竹里馆

独坐幽篁里，
弹琴复长啸。
深林人不知，
明月来相照。

Wangwei (701—761)

The Guest House in the Bamboos

Deep in the bamboo grove I sit alone,

I pluck the *qin*, cry a long melody;

In these unpeopled woods I sing unknown,

But the bright moon comes and shines on me.

王维 (701—761)

山居秋暝

空山新雨后,
天气晚来秋。
明月松间照,
清泉石上流。
竹喧归浣女,
莲动下渔舟。
随意春芳歇,
王孙自可留。

Wangwei (701—761)

Autumn Evening at Home in the Mountains

The mountain's empty after fresh rain,

Autumn permeates evening air;

A bright moon's shining through the needled pine,

Among the stones the spring flows pure and clear.

Girls come from washing rustle the bamboos,

Fishing-boats pass, lotuses sink and stir.

The sweet spring grass has withered—what of that?

This is a dwelling for I to stay.

王维(wáng wéi)(701—761)

终南山(zhōng nán shān)

太(tài)乙(yǐ)近(jìn)天(tiān)都(dū),

连(lián)山(shān)到(dào)海(hǎi)隅(yú)。

白(bái)云(yún)回(huí)望(wàng)合(hé),

青(qīng)霭(ǎi)入(rù)看(kàn)无(wú)。

分(fēn)野(yě)中(zhōng)峰(fēng)变(biàn),

阴(yīn)晴(qíng)众(zhòng)壑(hè)殊(shū)。

欲(yù)投(tóu)人(rén)处(chù)宿(sù),

隔(gé)水(shuǐ)问(wèn)樵(qiáo)夫(fū)。

Wangwei (701—761)

The Zhongnan Mountain

Close to Heaven's capital stands Mount Taiyi,

Its ranges reach the margins of the sea,

Its white clouds part before me, close behind;

I enter a blue haze I no longer see;

Across its peak the constellations change,

Its valleys lit or shadowed variously.

Across the river there's a woodman: he

May tell me where to find a hostelry.

王维(701—761)

汉江临眺

楚塞三湘接,
荆门九派通。
江流天地外,
山色有无中。
郡邑浮前浦,
波澜动远空。
襄阳好风日,
留醉与山翁。

Wangwei (701—761)

The Han River Seen from a High Vantage Point

The three Xiang forks join at the Chu frontier,

Through the Jing Gate nine streams pour to the sea;

The river flows far beyond earth and heaven,

The mountains seem to be and not to be;

Cities and realms float by the riverside,

Great billows roil the void immensity.

Ah yes, Xiangyang has pretty scenery:

I'll leave to drunk Old Shan the ecstasy!

王 维 (701—761)
渭川田家

斜光照墟落，
穷巷牛羊归。
野老念牧童，
倚杖候荆扉。
雉雊麦苗秀，
蚕眠桑叶稀。
田夫荷锄立，
相见语依依。
即此羡闲逸，
怅然吟式微。

Wangwei (701—761)

Peasants by the River Wei

Across the hamlet slants the evening light,

Cattle and sheep come ambling down the street,

An aged peasant waits for the herd boy,

Leans on his cane beside a wicker gate.

The pheasants whir in eared and ripening wheat,

In tattered mulberry leaves the silkworms drowse;

A farmer with a hoe comes by; they meet

And talk; no haste to part; the time allows.

I envy them their peaceful unconcern

And sadly chant "Some Day I Will Return."

王维 wáng wéi (701—761)

渭城曲 wèi chéng qǔ

渭城朝雨浥轻尘，
客舍青青柳色新。
劝君更尽一杯酒，
西出阳关无故人。

Wangwei (701—761)

Song of Weicheng City

The dawn rain lays the dust in Weicheng City,

Spring willow-light has greened the guest-house round;

My dearest sir, drain one more cup of wine;

West of Yang Pass no old friends can be found.

王维 (701—761)

鸟鸣涧

人闲桂花落，
夜静春山空。
月出惊山鸟，
时鸣春涧中。

Wangwei (701—761)

Birds Singing in the Ravine

I am quite still. Osmanthus flowers fall.

The spring night's quiet, the mountain is serene.

The moon comes out, alarms mountain birds.

At times he sings down in the spring ravine.

王维(701—761)
wáng wéi

终南别业
zhōng nán bié yè

中岁颇好道,
zhōng suì pō hào dào

晚家南山陲。
wǎn jiā nán shān chuí

兴来每独往,
xìng lái měi dú wǎng

胜事空自知。
shèng shì kōng zì zhī

行到水穷处,
xíng dào shuǐ qióng chù

坐看云起时。
zuò kàn yún qǐ shí

偶然值林叟,
ǒu rán zhí lín sǒu

谈笑无还期。
tán xiào wú huán qī

Wangwei (701—761)

The Villa of Mount Zhongnan

In middle age I came to love the Dao,

In old age dwell now under Mount Zhongnan.

The mood comes often to go out alone;

There's good only the empty self can know.

I walk beside the water to its bourne,

And there I sit and watch the rising clouds.

Sometimes I meet an old man in the woods:

We talk and laugh with no thought of return.

王维(701—761)

酬张少府

晚年惟好静，
万事不关心。
自顾无长策，
空知返旧林。
松风吹解带，
山月照弹琴。
君问穷通理，
渔歌入浦深。

Wangwei (701—761)

In Return for a Poem from Deputy Prefect Zhang

Now late in years, stillness is all I crave.

Free of "ten thousand things" my heart's at ease.

I see myself as one with no designs,

Know only the way back among the trees.

The pine-borne breeze has blown my sash undone;

The mountain moon lights my *qin's* melodies.

You ask the truth of failure and success:

From river-deeps a fisher's song replies.

lǐ bái
李 白(701—762)

zèng wāng lún
赠 汪 伦

李白乘舟将欲行,
忽闻岸上踏歌声。
桃花潭水深千尺,
不及汪伦送我情。

Libai (701—762)

For Wang Lun

Li Bai has got aboard his boat,
   his journey will be long;

Upon the bank he hears the sound
   of footsteps and of song.

The Peach-Tree Lake is deep, so deep,
   a thousand feet wellnigh,

But not as deep as Wang Lun's heart
   As he bids me goodbye.

李 白 (701—762)

静夜思

床前明月光，
疑是地上霜。
举头望明月，
低头思故乡。

Libai (701—762)

Thoughts in a Silent Night

The moonlight falling by my bed tonight

I took for early frost upon the ground.

I lift my head, gaze at the moon, so bright,

I lower my head, think of my native land.

李白(701—762)

渡荆门送别

渡远荆门外，
来从楚国游。
山随平野尽，
江入大荒流。
月下飞天镜，
云生结海楼。
仍怜故乡水，
万里送行舟。

Libai (701—762)

Farewell, Upon Passing Mount Jingmen

And now at length I've passed beyond Jingmen

On my adventure to the land of Chu.

The mountains end, the flatlands open out,

The Yangtze meets the vast plains and pours through.

The moon is flung upon its heavenly mirror,

The clouds grow mirages of towers and sea;

But still I love the waters of my homeland

That travel with my boat a thousand *li*.

李 白（701—762）

登金陵凤凰台

凤凰台上凤凰游，
凤去台空江自流。
吴宫花草埋幽径，
晋代衣冠成古丘。
三山半落青天外，
二水中分白鹭洲。
总为浮云能蔽日，
长安不见使人愁。

Libai (701—762)

Ascending the Phoenix Tower of Jinling

Once on the Phoenix Tower played
    the fabled phoenix shrill,

That bird is gone, the tower stands void,
    the river flows on still.

In the Wu Palace grass and flowers
    choke deep the rutted way;

Fine nobles of the house of Jin
    leave nothing but a hill.

The Three-Peak Mountain falls beyond
    the blue rim of the sky,

The double river parts around
    the far White Egret Isle;

Always gross veils of cloud may hide
    the glorious sun of heaven—

Royal Chang'an is hid from sight,
    and my heart feels the chill.

李白 (701—762)

蜀道难

噫吁嚱，
危乎高哉！
蜀道之难，
难于上青天！
蚕丛及鱼凫，
开国何茫然！
尔来四万八千岁，
不与秦塞通人烟。
西当太白有鸟道，
可以横绝峨眉巅。

Libai (701—762)

The Perilous Shu Road

Ah, terrible, that road!

How dangerous, how high!

The road to Shu is the most dreadful way,

Harder to climb than is the deep blue sky.

The realms of Can Cong and Yu Fu go back

To foundings lost to human memory;

Forty-eight thousand years since then they
   let go drifting by

But never with the forts of Qin
   shared message or reply.

The west of Mount Taibai
   is where the wild birds fly,

Migrants that find their way across
   the summit of Emei.

第一部分 唐诗

地崩山摧壮士死，
然后天梯石栈相钩连。
上有六龙回日之高标，
下有冲波逆折之回川。
黄鹤之飞尚不得过，
猿猱欲度愁攀援。
青泥何盘盘，
百步九折萦岩峦。
扪参历井仰胁息，
以手抚膺坐长叹。
问君西游何时还？
畏途巉岩不可攀。

It's said the mountain broke and fell

    in a great landslide

    and many brave men died

And afterward the stair of heaven was joined

    to the cliff causeway.

Above, a peak so high

    the six swift dragons of the sun must veer aside;

Below, a rushing flood whose churning waves

    turn back in whirlpools on themselves.

Even the yellow crane can not fly over,

The very apes wish they could cross but fear to climb.

So spiraled round is Qingni Pinnacle,

To climb a hundred steps takes nine

    whole circuits of the stone;

You touch Orion, Gemini,

    you look up, hold your breath—

You stroke your overburdened chest

—you heave a long deep sigh.

I ask you, traveler in the West,

    when, sir, will you return?

但见悲鸟号古木,
雄飞雌从绕林间。
又闻子规啼夜月,
愁空山。
蜀道之难,
难于上青天,
使人听此凋朱颜!
连峰去天不盈尺,
枯松倒挂倚绝壁。
飞湍瀑流争喧豗,
砯崖转石万壑雷。
其险也如此,
嗟尔远道之人胡为乎来哉!

That dreadful road, those towering cliffs—
　　you cannot pass that way,
Where in the old trees the birds
　　scream out their grieving cry,
And through primeval forest shades
　　the males, then females, fly;
The cuckoo, too, mourns its sad lullaby,
The haunted moon in empty mountains high.
The road to Shu is the most dreadful way,
Harder to climb than is the deep blue sky.
That youthful bloom, you who hear this,
　　well may it turn to grey!
Scarcely a foot away from heaven
　　there hangs a withered pine,
That clings against a precipice
　　twisted and upside down.
The flying torrents, waterfalls,
　　strive in a rumbling roar,
Ten thousand avalanches crash
　　in chasms far and near.
If then so perilous as it is here,
Ah, you who travel from so far away,

剑阁峥嵘而崔嵬,
一夫当关,
万夫莫开。
所守或匪亲,
化为狼与豺。
朝避猛虎,
夕避长蛇;
磨牙吮血,
杀人如麻。
锦城虽云乐,
不如早还家。
蜀道之难,
难于上青天,
侧身西望长咨嗟!

What reason brings you hither, why, O why?

The pass of Jiange climbs among
　　steep towers to the sky,

If one man guards the narrow way,
　　ten thousand can't get by;

Whoever guards it must be trustworthy

Lest he will become the wolf's and jackal's prey.

Shun the tiger in the dawn,

In the night shun the reptiles;

Grinding tooth and bloody yawn

Many many lives do take.

Though pleasures can be found in Brocade Town

You're better off at home, for your own sake.

The road to Shu is the most dreadful way,

Harder to climb than is the deep blue sky.

I turn toward the distant west,
　　and heave a long deep sigh!

李白(701—762)

早发白帝城

朝辞白帝彩云间,
千里江陵一日还。
两岸猿声啼不住,
轻舟已过万重山。

Libai (701—762)

Early Start from White King City

I leave Baidi in its white clouds,
　　at dawn I'm on my way,
To Jiangling it's a thousand *li*,
　　but it will take one day.
The screaming monkeys on the banks
　　will never cease their calls;
My light boat has already passed
　　ten thousand mountain-walls!

李 白（701—762）

丁都护歌

云阳上征去，
两岸饶商贾。
吴牛喘月时，
拖船一何苦！
水浊不可饮，
壶浆半成土。
一唱都护歌，
心摧泪如雨。
万人凿盘石，
无由达江浒。
君看石芒砀，
掩泪悲千古！

Libai (701—762)

Song of Frontier Commander Ding

Upstream from Yunyang, both banks when you go

Are lined with wealthy businesses. Oh,

When the Wu oxen gasp against the moon,

What toil to drag the boats against the flow!

When the foul water is not fit to drink,

A pot of tea is half mud down below,

Then when we sing the work-song of "Du Hu"

Our heartsick tears like raindrops overflow.

Ten thousand men haul at tethered rocks,

But can we get it to the river? No.

Sir, if you saw those ponderous huge stones,

You must forever hide your tears of woe!

李白 (701—762)

长干行

妾发初覆额,
折花门前剧。
郎骑竹马来,
绕床弄青梅。
同居长干里,
两小无嫌猜。
十四为君妇,
羞颜未尝开。
低头向暗壁,

Libai (701—762)

Song of Changgan

When my first fringe fell down across my forehead,

I picked a flower, played before the door.

Riding a bamboo horse, my love, you found me,

We chased green plums around the well fence.

We dwelt close by in Changgan's lanes and alleys,

Two small folk with no guile, in perfect peace.

When I was fourteen I became your wife, sir,

But being shy, I refused to show my face.

I turned my head toward the wall and would not,

千唤不一回。
十五始展眉，
愿同尘与灰。
常存抱柱信，
岂上望夫台。
十六君远行，
瞿塘滟滪堆。
五月不可触，
猿声天上哀。
门前迟行迹，
一一生绿苔。
苔深不能扫，

Though called a thousand times, give any sign.

Only at fifteen I unclenched my eyebrows,

Willed that my dust be ever mixed with thine.

And I embraced the "pillar of pure trusting",

Why climb the roof-walk, spy what you might do?

At sixteen, sir, you left on a long voyage,

Past the dread Yanyu reefs and Qutang Gorge.

In May I prayed you had not struck the rocks, love,

The very apes would wail in grief for you.

I still can see your tracks beside the doorway.

But now they're almost covered up with moss

So deep, it is forbidden now to sweep them,

luò yè qiū fēng zǎo
落 叶 秋 风 早。

bā yuè hú dié huáng
八 月 蝴 蝶 黄,

shuāng fēi xī yuán cǎo
双 飞 西 园 草。

gǎn cǐ shāng qiè xīn
感 此 伤 妾 心,

zuò chóu hóng yán lǎo
坐 愁 红 颜 老。

zǎo wǎn xià sān bā
早 晚 下 三 巴,

yù jiāng shū bào jiā
预 将 书 报 家。

xiāng yíng bù dào yuǎn
相 迎 不 道 远,

zhí zhì cháng fēng shā
直 至 长 风 沙。

And early autumn winds blow leaves across.

In August two bright butterflies together

Fluttered above the western garden grass;

It hurts me that my heart is full of worry,

My pretty face grows old within the glass.

When you come down through Sanba①, write to me and tell me

How soon you're coming home, and how you are,

And I'll come out and meet you on your journey,

Even if it's as far as Changfengsha.

---

① Places referring to Ba county, the east and west part of Ba County; almost the eastern part of Sichuan Province.

李 白 (701—762)

将进酒

君不见黄河之水天上来，
奔流到海不复回。
君不见高堂明镜悲白发，
朝如青丝暮成雪。
人生得意须尽欢，
莫使金樽空对月。
天生我材必有用，
千金散尽还复来。
烹羊宰牛且为乐，

Libai (701—762)

Bring in the Wine: a Drinking Song

Can't you see the Yellow River gushing from the overwhelming sky,

Pouring to the ocean always, never to return?

Can't you see the shining mirror, grieving in the high hall for your hair,

Silken black at dawn, that dusk has turned to snow?

If your fortune favors, drink up all the joy,

Do not let the golden wine-cup in the moonlight ever yet run dry.

Always shall my heaven-born genius find a way to serve;

Let a thousand coins of gold be scattered, easy come and easy go;

Let us kill the fatted lamb, the ox, and celebrate the moment,

huì xū yī yǐn sān bǎi bēi
会须一饮三百杯。

cén fū zǐ dān qiū shēng
岑夫子，丹丘生，

qiāng jìn jiǔ bēi mò tíng
将进酒，杯莫停。

yǔ jūn gē yī qǔ
与君歌一曲，

qǐng jūn wèi wǒ qīng ěr tīng
请君为我倾耳听。

zhōng gǔ zhuàn yù bù zú guì
钟鼓馔玉不足贵，

dàn yuàn cháng zuì bù fù xǐng
但愿长醉不复醒。

gǔ lái shèng xián jiē jì mò
古来圣贤皆寂寞，

wéi yǒu yǐn zhě liú qí míng
惟有饮者留其名。

chén wáng xī shí yàn píng lè
陈王昔时宴平乐，

dǒu jiǔ shí qiān zì huān xuè
斗酒十千恣欢谑。

zhǔ rén hé wèi yán shǎo qián
主人何为言少钱，

jìng xū gū qǔ duì jūn zhuó
径须沽取对君酌。

wǔ huā mǎ qiān jīn qiú
五花马，千金裘，

hū ér jiāng chū huàn měi jiǔ
呼儿将出换美酒，

yǔ ěr tóng xiāo wàn gǔ chóu
与尔同销万古愁。

Let us drink three hundred healths at but one sitting!

Master Chen the Scholar! Yuan Danqiu the learned student!

Bring the wine in! Never cease the drinking!

Listen now, for I shall sing a song.

Bell and drum and jade and every dainty delicacy are not sweet enough:

Let us but be drunk and never wake again.

Virtuous and holy sages since the ancient times have vanished, not to leave a name;

Only the great drunkards live in memory:

Lord Chen once gave a banquet at the Pingle Temple

Where they drank a tun of wine that cost ten thousand— let us, as they did, drink and be as merry.

Master of the revels, why should you care about the money?

Go and pay the vintner, face him down and pour the good wine forth—

Take my darling flower-dappled horse, my coat that cost a thousand,

Call the boy, and sell them all to buy the shining wine.

And as for you and I, may our ten thousand endless griefs be drowned in that good wine.

李 白（701—762）

月下独酌·其一

花间一壶酒，
独酌无相亲。
举杯邀明月，
对影成三人。
月既不解饮，
影徒随我身。
暂伴月将影，
行乐须及春。
我歌月徘徊，
我舞影零乱。
醒时同交欢，
醉后各分散。
永结无情游，
相期邈云汉。

Libai (701—762)

Drinking Alone Under the Moon (No.1)

Among the flowers with one lone jug of wine

I drink without a friend to drink with me.

But I'll lift up my cup, invite the moon,

So with my shadow we will make up three.

The moon's immune, though, to debauchery,

And my poor shadow follows me in vain;

Still, Moon and Shadow are my company—

The joys of spring may never come again.

So as I sing, Moon wanders aimlessly,

And as I dance, poor tangled Shadow reels;

Sober, we were in perfect harmony,

Now, drunk, there's no connection of our heels;

But, careless of this world, we're bound, one day,

To meet together in the Milky Way.

李白 (701—762)

行路难·其一

金樽清酒斗十千,
玉盘珍羞直万钱。
停杯投箸不能食,
拔剑四顾心茫然。
欲渡黄河冰塞川,
将登太行雪满山。
闲来垂钓碧溪上,
忽复乘舟梦日边。
行路难,行路难,
多歧路,今安在?
长风破浪会有时,
直挂云帆济沧海。

Libai (701—762)

In Difficulty (No. 1)

Gold goblets of good wine can cost
   a thousand for one quart,
Ten thousand for a fine jade dish
   of dainties served at court;
But stop the cup, throw chopsticks out,
   I have no will to eat;
I draw my sword, look wildly round,
   perplexed and sick at heart.

I'd cross the Yellow River but
   the water's clogged with ice;
I'd climb Mount Taihang but the snow
   darkens the lowering skies.
Like one who waits for miracles
   idly I fish the brook,
Have sudden dreams that I've set sail
   toward a bright sunrise.
But I am stranded, caught!
   But I am trapped and caught!
So many forking ways, which one
   is the right path for me?
To ride the wind and cleave the waves
   the time will come unsought;
I'll hoist my sail up to the clouds
   and cross the deep blue sea!

李白 (701—762)

宣州谢朓楼饯别校书叔云

弃我去者,
昨日之日不可留;
乱我心者,
今日之日多烦忧。
长风万里送秋雁,
对此可以酣高楼。
蓬莱文章建安骨,
中间小谢又清发。
俱怀逸兴壮思飞,
欲上青天揽明月。
抽刀断水水更流,
举杯消愁愁更愁。
人生在世不称意,
明朝散发弄扁舟。

Libai (701—762)

The Poet's Farewell Dinner for His Uncle, Secretary Li Yun, in the Xie Tiao Tower of Xuanzhou

O how could it abandon me
   the day that happened yesterday,
   that no one can retain—
O why shakes so this
heart in me
   the day that's happening today,
   so full of grief and pain!
Ten thousand *li* of autumn wind
   bid the wild geese farewell,
We see it from the storied tower,
   and drink and drink again.
Your writings, in the "Elfland" school,
   strong-boned, like old Jian An's,
And mine, like Xie the Younger's,
   drawn to a fresh clarity,
Both cherish a bold eagerness,
   a splendid urge to fly,
To climb the blue wind and embrace
   the bright moon in the sky.
I draw my sword, I cut the flood,
   the waters yet flow on;
I raise the cup to melt my griefs,
   but pain piles up on pain;
Man's life in this world thwarts desire,
   my wishes are but vain:
Tomorrow I'll undo my hair,
   take out my boat again.

李 白 (701—762)

长相思·其一

长相思，在长安。
络纬秋啼金井阑，
微霜凄凄簟色寒。
孤灯不明思欲绝，
卷帷望月空长叹。
美人如花隔云端！
上有青冥之长天，
下有渌水之波澜。
天长路远魂飞苦，
梦魂不到关山难。
长相思，摧心肝！

Libai (701—762)

Long Have I Longed for You (No.1)

Long have I longed for you
   Here in the capital.
Beside the golden well-rail sing
   the katydids of Fall,
A light frost chills the sleeping-mat,
   its color cold and dull.
The solitary lamp is dim,
   my thoughts drag to their end,
I furl the drape, gaze at the moon,
   sigh vainly at it all.

Beauty's a flower in the clouds,
   distant, untouchable!
Above, the sky, so vast, so high,
   stretches empyreal;
Below, the waters, wild and pure,
   in great waves surge and fall.
The sky is wide, the earth is far,
   in pain the spirit flies;
The mountain passes bar the way
   against my dreaming soul.
Long have I longed for you!
Heart breaks, it is too full.

李白 (701—762)

塞下曲·其一

五月天山雪,
无花只有寒。
笛中闻折柳,
春色未曾看。
晓战随金鼓,
宵眠抱玉鞍。
愿将腰下剑,
直为斩楼兰。

Libai (701—762)

Songs of the Frontier Fortress (No. 1)

It snows in May up in the high Tianshan;

There are no flowers, there is only cold;

The tune of "Broken Willow" on a flute;

No sign of springtime's pink and green and gold.

We rise at dawn with gong and drum to fight;

We sleep at night, jade saddles in our hold;

The good sword at my side, and iron-souled,

To slay Loulan I march out hot and bold.

李白(701—762)

梦游天姥吟留别

海客谈瀛洲,
烟涛微茫信难求。
越人语天姥,
云霞明灭或可睹。
天姥连天向天横,
势拔五岳掩赤城。
天台四万八千丈,
对此欲倒东南倾。
我欲因之梦吴越,
一夜飞度镜湖月。

Libai (701—762)

Dream Journey on Mount Tianmu: a Farewell Song

Seafarers tell the legend of Yingzhou,

Fair isle so hard to find amid
 the misty billows' flow;

Likewise in Yue men speak of Mount Tianmu,

That in dark clouds or rainbows bright
 glides sometimes into view.

Tianmu's so high that it touches heaven,
 so wide it lines the sky,

Its sweep surpasses the Five Peaks,
 hides Chicheng from the eye.

Mount Tiantai's half-a-million feet
 toppling, seem not so high,

Bowing toward great Tianmu's seat
 in the south-eastern sky.

Fired by this vision, one night I
 dreamed of the land of Yue;

I'm flying over Mirror Lake,
 where the bright moon holds sway;

湖月照我影，
送我至剡溪。
谢公宿处今尚在，
渌水荡漾清猿啼。
脚著谢公屐，
身登青云梯。
半壁见海日，
空中闻天鸡。
千岩万转路不定，
迷花倚石忽已暝。
熊咆龙吟殷岩泉，
栗深林兮惊层巅。
云青青兮欲雨，

That bright moon casts my shadow on the lake
And ushers me toward the clear Shan Rill
Where dwelt the poet-master Xie,
   and his old home is still,
And over the pure ripples wail
   the apes' cries, sad and shrill.

I don the simple clogs of Master Xie,
My body climbs the blue cloud ladder way;
Half up the cliff, look, sunrise on the sea,
And listen, for the cock crows in the day.

Ten thousand rocks, ten thousand turns,
   the unfixed path winds on;
Tranced by a flower, till sudden dark
   I lean against a stone.
With roars of bears and dragon-screams
   and rumbling waterfalls
I tremble at the forests deep,
   the layered mountain-walls:
Ai! These blue blue clouds
   full of the coming rain!
Ai! These pale pale waters,
   from which the white mist crawls!

水澹澹兮生烟。
列缺霹雳，
丘峦崩摧。
洞天石扉，
訇然中开。
青冥浩荡不见底，
日月照耀金银台。
霓为衣兮风为马，
云之君兮纷纷而来下。
虎鼓瑟兮鸾回车，
仙之人兮列如麻。
忽魂悸以魄动，
恍惊起而长嗟。

Now there's a sudden thunderbolt,

A landslip slumps down from a fault!

There the stone gates of fairyland

Crash open now on either hand,

Reveal a vast and teal-green space,

 a fathomless sky-vault

Where in the sun and moonlight, gold

 and silver towers stand.

Their clothes are glowing rainbows, Ai!

 Their horses, the wild wind;

The gods of cloud, Ai! See their glittering files

 in endless multitudes descend!

The tiger strikes the zither, Ai!

 Those phoenix charioteers!

Ai! See how the Immortal Ones

 their serried ranks extend!

My heart is quaking, Ai!

 My unquiet heart is stirred;

Ah, in this sudden terror

 I wake with a long sigh.

惟觉时之枕席，
失向来之烟霞。
世间行乐亦如此，
古来万事东流水。
别君去兮何时还？
且放白鹿青崖间，
须行即骑访名山。
安能摧眉折腰事权贵，
使我不得开心颜！

What's left, alas, is only
　　a pillow and a mat;
Oh, where is that bright mist now?
　　Where is that rosy cloud?
Thus all the pleasures of the world
　　are transient as a dream,
Passing forever from the earth
　　as rivers eastward stream.

Farewell, my friend; I do not know
　　the time of my return;
For now I'll let my white stag graze
　　in these cliffs green with fern—
If called, I'll reascend that peak
　　upon his swift back borne;
But how shall I with lowered brow
　　and bent neck to the mighty turn,
Where there's no opening of face or heart,
　　in service to their scorn?

高适 (702—765)

别董大

千里黄云白日曛，
北风吹雁雪纷纷。
莫愁前路无知己，
天下谁人不识君。

Gaoshi (702—765)

Farewell to Mr. Dong, the Eldest Son of the Family

A thousand *li* of yellow cloud,
　the dim sun's whitish glow;
The north wind blows a flurry of
　wild geese and wilder snow.
Fear not that on the road ahead
　no soul mate may be found:
For under heaven who is he
　that your name does not know?

崔颢(cuī hào)(704?—754)

黄鹤楼(huáng hè lóu)

昔(xī)人(rén)已(yǐ)乘(chéng)黄(huáng)鹤(hè)去(qù),
此(cǐ)地(dì)空(kōng)余(yú)黄(huáng)鹤(hè)楼(lóu)。
黄(huáng)鹤(hè)一(yī)去(qù)不(bù)复(fù)返(fǎn),
白(bái)云(yún)千(qiān)载(zǎi)空(kōng)悠(yōu)悠(yōu)。
晴(qíng)川(chuān)历(lì)历(lì)汉(hàn)阳(yáng)树(shù),
芳(fāng)草(cǎo)萋(qī)萋(qī)鹦(yīng)鹉(wǔ)洲(zhōu)。
日(rì)暮(mù)乡(xiāng)关(guān)何(hé)处(chù)是(shì)?
烟(yān)波(bō)江(jiāng)上(shàng)使(shǐ)人(rén)愁(chóu)。

Cuihao (704?—754)

Yellow Crane Tower

The fay who rode the yellow crane
    long ago passed away;

The Tower of the Yellow Crane
    stands empty to this day.

The magic yellow crane, once gone,
    no longer reappears;

Only this vast white lonely cloud
    looms through a thousand years!

The sunlit river and the trees
    of Han Yang clear and bright,

The sweet grass, lush on Parrot Isle
    lie spread out in the light.

But evening comes, and night will fall;
    where is my native gate?

The mist upon the water grieves
    my soul, and it grows late!

崔颢 (704?—754)

长干行·其一

君家何处住，

妾住在横塘。

停船暂借问，

或恐是同乡。

Cuihao (704?—754)

Songs of Changgan (No.1)

Where do you come from, sir, if I might ask?

This maiden lives beside the Pool of Heng.

Please stop your boat a moment; if we're neighbors

To pass by would be an unlucky thing.

崔颢（704?—754）

长干行·其二

家临九江水，
来去九江侧。
同是长干人，
生小不相识。

Cuihao (704?—754)

Songs of Changgan (No. 2)

My home looks out upon the Jiujiang's waters,

I come and go upon the broad Jiujiang.

Indeed we're both from Changgan, as you mentioned,

But did not meet, I think, when we were young.

杜甫(712—770)

绝句四首·其三

两个黄鹂鸣翠柳,

一行白鹭上青天。

窗含西岭千秋雪,

门泊东吴万里船。

Dufu (712—770)

Four Quatrains (No.3)

A pair of yellow orioles
  sing in the emerald willow;

A line of herons, brilliant white,
  soar in the pure blue sky.

The window's mouth frames the West Range—
  a thousand years of snow;

Moored by the water gate East Wu's
  ten thousand small craft lie.

杜甫 (712—770)

望岳

岱宗夫如何？
齐鲁青未了。
造化钟神秀，
阴阳割昏晓。
荡胸生层云，
决眦入归鸟。
会当凌绝顶，
一览众山小。

Dufu (712—770)

Distant View of the Great Mountain

What is there like you, reverend Mount Tai?

To north and south spread out an endless green;

Here heaven and earth join miracle with grace,

Your dawn and dusk slopes split the Yang and Yin.

My heart rinsed by your growing layers of cloud,

My eyes pierced by the homing birds they've seen,

I must at last climb to the very peak,

And see all lesser hills that there have been.

杜 甫(712—770)

春夜喜雨

好雨知时节,
当春乃发生。
随风潜入夜,
润物细无声。
野径云俱黑,
江船火独明。
晓看红湿处,
花重锦官城。

Dufu (712—770)

Spring Night with Happy Rain

A good rain knows the season when it's right,

In spring, on time, it makes things sprout and grow.

Follow the wind, sneak out into the night:

All moist things whisper silently and slow.

Above the wild path, black clouds fill the air,

The boat-lamp on the flood the only glow;

At dawn you see wet mounds of crimson where

The heavy flowers of Chengdu hang down low.

杜 甫(dù fǔ)(712—770)

春望(chūn wàng)

国(guó) 破(pò) 山(shān) 河(hé) 在(zài),
城(chéng) 春(chūn) 草(cǎo) 木(mù) 深(shēn)。
感(gǎn) 时(shí) 花(huā) 溅(jiàn) 泪(lèi),
恨(hèn) 别(bié) 鸟(niǎo) 惊(jīng) 心(xīn)。
烽(fēng) 火(huǒ) 连(lián) 三(sān) 月(yuè),
家(jiā) 书(shū) 抵(dǐ) 万(wàn) 金(jīn)。
白(bái) 头(tóu) 搔(sāo) 更(gèng) 短(duǎn),
浑(hún) 欲(yù) 不(bú) 胜(shèng) 簪(zān)。

Dufu (712—770)

Spring: Gazing into the Distance

Shattered the state, but hill and stream live on;

Spring in the city, thick grows grass and tree.

I sigh the times, the flowers are splashed with tears;

A bird can fright the homesick heart in me.

The beacon fires have burned three months on end,

Letters from home weigh as ten thousand gold;

I rub my white head till the hair's so thin

The pin that clasps it now will barely hold.

杜甫(dù fǔ)(712—770)

前出塞九首·其六

挽弓当挽强,
用箭当用长。
射人先射马,
擒贼先擒王。
杀人亦有限,
列国自有疆。
苟能制侵陵,
岂在多杀伤。

Dufu (712—770)

Beyond the Frontier Pass (No. 6)

Who bends a bow should bend one that is strong;

Who draws an arrow, choose one that is long.

If you would shoot a man, first shoot his horse;

To take the enemy, first take their king.

But there must be some end to slaughtering;

All nations have their own distinct frontiers:

If we can check aggressive bullying,

What need for so much killing, harm, and wrong?

杜甫（712—770）

蜀相

丞相祠堂何处寻，
锦官城外柏森森。
映阶碧草自春色，
隔叶黄鹂空好音。
三顾频烦天下计，
两朝开济老臣心。
出师未捷身先死，
长使英雄泪满襟。

Dufu (712—770)

The Shu Prime Minister

Where is that noble minister's
  commemorative shrine?
Outside the Brocade City, in
  dark cypress-groves, alone.
Stone stairways mirror blue-green grass,
  unkempt in this spring scene;
A yellow oriole, hid in fronds,
  sings sweetly, but in vain.

Three times the nation called on him
  to serve it by his art;
Two empires the old minister
  guided with all his heart;
He led the troops to victory,
  but died before they won—
Which wets with tears the garments of
  heroic gentlemen.

杜甫(dù fǔ) (712—770)

兵车行(bīng chē xíng)

车(chē)辚(lín)辚(lín)，马(mǎ)萧(xiāo)萧(xiāo)，
行(xíng)人(rén)弓(gōng)箭(jiàn)各(gè)在(zài)腰(yāo)。
爷(yé)娘(niáng)妻(qī)子(zǐ)走(zǒu)相(xiāng)送(sòng)，
尘(chén)埃(āi)不(bù)见(jiàn)咸(xián)阳(yáng)桥(qiáo)。
牵(qiān)衣(yī)顿(dùn)足(zú)拦(lán)道(dào)哭(kū)，
哭(kū)声(shēng)直(zhí)上(shàng)干(gān)云(yún)霄(xiāo)。
道(dào)旁(páng)过(guò)者(zhě)问(wèn)行(xíng)人(rén)，
行(xíng)人(rén)但(dàn)云(yún)点(diǎn)行(háng)频(pín)。
或(huò)从(cóng)十(shí)五(wǔ)北(běi)防(fáng)河(hé)，
便(biàn)至(zhì)四(sì)十(shí)西(xī)营(yíng)田(tián)。

Dufu (712—770)

Song of the War Chariots

Chariot-wheels scream,

   the horses wildly neigh;

With bows and arrows on their backs

   the conscripts make their way;

Where fathers, mothers, children, wives,

   run out to see them go,

The Xianyang Bridge is dark with dust

   although it is broad day;

They snatch at coats, shriek, stamp their feet,

   and try to block the road,

The cry goes up and strikes the clouds—

   Heaven's in disarray.

A passerby along the way

   questions the conscript band;

The men can only say they have

   been drafted many times.

Some, at fifteen, were sent up north

   to guard the river, and

At forty, ordered to the west

   to break the new ploughland.

去时里正与裹头，
归来头白还戍边。
边庭流血成海水，
武皇开边意未已。
君不闻汉家山东二百州，
千村万落生荆杞。
纵有健妇把锄犁，
禾生陇亩无东西。
况复秦兵耐苦战，
被驱不异犬与鸡。
长者虽有问，
役夫敢申恨？
且如今年冬，

The village chieftain when he left

 helped tie his head-band here;

That head was white when he returned,

 still—back to the frontier.

Out at the front the soldiers shed

 an ocean of their blood;

Emperor Wu will never cease

 to make his conquests good.

"Haven't you heard, sir? In the realms of Han

 east of Mount Hua, two hundred prefectures,

There are ten thousand villages

 where only thorns now grow.

Even if sturdy women can

 handle the plow and hoe,

The dike-divisions of the grain

 unsquared, to chaos go.

The bravest warriors of the Qin

 Who've borne the brunt of war,

Like dogs or chickens yet are driven."

Although you, reverend sir, inquire, how dare,

A mere recruit speak out his fierce despair?

Just take this winter, when they wouldn't give,

未休关西卒。
县官急索租，
租税从何出？
信知生男恶，
反是生女好。
生女犹得嫁比邻，
生男埋没随百草。
君不见，青海头，
古来白骨无人收。
新鬼烦冤旧鬼哭，
天阴雨湿声啾啾！

The western garrison their rest and leave.

The local bosses want their rent, but yet

Where does rent come from? —that's what they forget.

To have a boy is bad luck nowadays,

A girl is good luck, such now are the ways.

Marry her to the man next door

    and let the matter pass,

Your boy, though, will lie buried far

    under the blowing grass.

"Haven't you seen, old sir,

    up by the Blue Lake's head,

Since ancient times ungathered lie the bleached

    bones of the dead?

The new ghosts rage in bitterness,

    the old ghosts weep and sigh;

In rain or under cloud-dark sky,

    like birds they cry and cry."

杜 甫 (712—770)

对 雪

战哭多新鬼，
愁吟独老翁。
乱云低薄暮，
急雪舞回风。
瓢弃尊无绿，
炉存火似红。
数州消息断，
愁坐正书空。

Dufu (712—770)

Facing the Snow

Many new ghosts cry out, in battle slain;

An old man's chanting, anxious and alone.

Chaotic clouds oppress the setting sun,

Windblown, a rush of dancing snow spins down.

The gourd's abandoned by the dry wine-jar,

The stove is real, flames seem to burn again.

The mails are cut, through several prefectures;

I sit here, anxious, write on the air in vain.

杜甫(712—770)

茅屋为秋风所破歌

八月秋高风怒号,
卷我屋上三重茅。
茅飞渡江洒江郊,
高者挂罥长林梢,
下者飘转沉塘坳。
南村群童欺我老无力,
忍能对面为盗贼。
公然抱茅入竹去,
唇焦口燥呼不得,
归来倚杖自叹息。

Dufu (712—770)

Thatched Cottage Wrecked by Autumn Gales: a Song

From August's tall sky with a howl
   a gale began to blow;

It rolled the thatch right off my house,
   three layers in a row.

The straw flew up and sprinkled on
   the river bank below:

The higher part hung up on twigs
   where the dense thickets grow;

The lower part swirled floating down,
   sank in the pool's deep flow.

From the South Village crowds of children came
   to bully this feeble old man.

Hard-hearted, they would play the thief
   brazenly to my face;

They picked the thatch up in their arms,
   fled in the thick bamboo.

With chapped lips and with hoarse dry throat
   I cried aloud in vain:

Returning, drew a heavy sigh
   and leaned upon my cane.

俄顷风定云墨色，
秋天漠漠向昏黑。
布衾多年冷似铁，
娇儿恶卧踏里裂。
床头屋漏无干处，
雨脚如麻未断绝。
自经丧乱少睡眠，
长夜沾湿何由彻！
安得广厦千万间，
大庇天下寒士俱欢颜！
风雨不动安如山。
呜呼！何时眼前突兀见此屋，
吾庐独破受冻死亦足！

At once the wind dropped, and the clouds
 turned inky in the murk,
The twilight of the autumn sky
 dimmed swiftly into black.
My cotton quilt through many years
 has turned as chill as iron,
By my dear boy in awkward sleep
 its lining kicked and torn.
On every bed the house now leaks,
 not one place is still dry,
The thickset stalks of rain, like hemp,
 uncut, still multiply.
Since the old Time of Troubles, I
 have not slept through the night;
How shall I hold out now, soaked through,
 until the morning light?
O for ten thousand thousand halls,
 ten thousand mansions wide,
Great shelter for poor scholars everywhere,
 with joyful faces, safe inside,
In wind and rain as still and sound
 as mountain fortified!
Ah me, if such a noble dwelling-place should tower
 before the poets gaping, open-eyed,
Then though my hut alone were wrecked, and I
 lie cold, I would die satisfied!

杜甫 (712—770)

赠花卿

锦城丝管日纷纷，
半入江风半入云。
此曲只应天上有，
人间能得几回闻。

Dufu (712—770)

For My Dear Friend Hua

In Chengdu strings and woodwinds play
　　ceaselessly day by day.

Half of it charms the river breeze,
　　half, the clouds of the sky.

Perhaps these notes should be reserved
　　only for heaven on high;

How many times can human
　　ears enjoy such stimuli?

杜 甫(712—770)

登岳阳楼

昔闻洞庭水，
今上岳阳楼。
吴楚东南坼，
乾坤日夜浮。
亲朋无一字，
老病有孤舟。
戎马关山北，
凭轩涕泗流。

Dufu (712—770)

Climbing the Tower of Yueyang

I heard once of Lake Dongting's endless waters,

I climb now Yueyang Tower to see this sight;

The lands of Wu and Chu split east and south;

Heaven and earth float here both day and night.

No word I hear from relatives or friends;

But one boat have I, I am old and ill;

North of Guanshan ride hostile cavalry;

I lean upon the rail, the thick tears fall.

杜甫(712—770)

旅夜书怀

细草微风岸,

危樯独夜舟。

星垂平野阔,

月涌大江流。

名岂文章著,

官应老病休。

飘飘何所似,

天地一沙鸥。

Dufu (712—770)

At Night Far From Home He Unburdens His Heart

A light wind in the thin grass of the shore,

A boat at night, tall-masted and alone;

The stars hang over a vast, open plain,

The moon swims in the mighty river's stream.

So, do my writings make a famous name?

This sick old officer should just resign.

Adrift, adrift, what kind of thing am I?

A lone white gull between the earth and sky.

杜 甫(712—770)

月 夜

今夜鄜州月，
闺中只独看。
遥怜小儿女，
未解忆长安。
香雾云鬟湿，
清辉玉臂寒。
何时倚虚幌，
双照泪痕干。

Dufu (712—770)

Moon and Night

Tonight the same moon stands above Fuzhou

My lady watches from her room, alone.

I yearn to hold my small son and my daughter,

Too young to know what happened in Chang'an.

Dampened with fog, my wife's black fragrant hair

Falls over jade-cold arms lit by the moon;

When will we lean upon the airy curtain

Together in this light, our tears dried? Soon?

杜甫(712—770)

石壕吏

暮投石壕村,
有吏夜捉人。
老翁逾墙走,
老妇出门看。
吏呼一何怒!
妇啼一何苦!
听妇前致词:
三男邺城戍。
一男附书至,
二男新战死。

Dufu (712—770)

The Sergeant of Stone Moat Village

I stayed one night in Stone Moat Village, when

They sent a sergeant to conscript a man;

But the old fellow climbed a wall and fled

And his wife kept the gateway while he ran.

The sergeant roared—he was so furious!

The old wife wept—her grief so piteous!

Hear her as she steps up to speak to him:

"To guard Yecheng they took three sons from us.

"We have received a letter from one son;

Both brothers died in battle, he lives on

存者且偷生，
死者长已矣！
室中更无人，
惟有乳下孙。
有孙母未去，
出入无完裙。
老妪力虽衰，
请从吏夜归。
急应河阳役，
犹得备晨炊。
夜久语声绝，
如闻泣幽咽。
天明登前途，
独与老翁别。

Dragging a meaningless existence still—

Then dead will not return, they're gone, they're gone!

"And there is no one left here to arrest,

Except a grandson at his mother's breast,

And she cannot yet leave the house, because

She has no clothes to go out fitly dressed.

"Sergeant, although I am a weak old dame,

Let me go with you now instead of them;

Right soon I'll answer to your call to arms,

I'll get your breakfast ready, there's still time."

The voices died, then a long silence fell;

Perhaps soft sobs and whimpers, I can't tell.

The sky got bright; I had to take the road;

Only to the old man I said farewell.

杜 甫 (712—770)

登 高

风急天高猿啸哀，
渚清沙白鸟飞回。
无边落木萧萧下，
不尽长江滚滚来。
万里悲秋常作客，
百年多病独登台。
艰难苦恨繁霜鬓，
潦倒新停浊酒杯。

Dufu (712—770)

Ascending a High Place

The wind is swift, the sky is high,
    apes give a long sad cry;

The water's clear, the isle's sand's white,
    the birds in circles fly.

Everywhere falling leaves swirl down,
    whistling in the gale;

Endless the river surges on
    in billows under sky.

Ten thousand *li* of somber fall
    a sojourner am I;

Aged by a hundred years of care
    I climb the tower alone.

Hard grief and bitter care have sowed
    thick hoarfrost in my hair;

I've given up my cup of wine,
    mud-tasting, in despair.

杜甫(712—770)

咏怀古迹五首·其三

群山万壑赴荆门,
生长明妃尚有村。
一去紫台连朔漠,
独留青冢向黄昏。
画图省识春风面,
环珮空归夜月魂。
千载琵琶作胡语,
分明怨恨曲中论。

Dufu (712—770)

Lament in Ancient Places (No. 3)

Ten thousand hills and valleys pour
    down to the Gates of Jin;

Here is the village Lady Ming
    was born and called her home.

Once you depart the Purple Halls
    you meet the northern waste;

A green tomb's all that's left of her
    lost in the yellow gloom.

The painting coarsely shows her face
    as fresh as the spring wind;

In jade and gold her soul returns
    in vain beneath the moon;

A thousand years her *Pipa* plays
    in a wild alien tongue;

Her grief can clearly be discerned
    in its reproachful tune.

杜甫(712—770)

客至

舍南舍北皆春水,
但见群鸥日日来。
花径不曾缘客扫,
蓬门今始为君开。
盘飧市远无兼味,
樽酒家贫只旧醅。
肯与邻翁相对饮,
隔篱呼取尽余杯。

Dufu (712—770)

My Guest Arrives

To north and south of my small house
    springs well up everywhere;

A flock of gulls is all you see,
    each day they fill the air.

Except for you, my dearest sir,
    the flowering path's unswept;

The wicker gate is open now,
    closed though it's always kept.

No fancy flavors grace our board,
    the market being far;

The wine in my poor home is but
    leftover in a jar;

What do you say, shall we invite
    the old man from next door?

I'll call over the fence to him
    to help us drink some more.

杜甫(712—770)

闻官军收河南河北

剑外忽传收蓟北，
初闻涕泪满衣裳。
却看妻子愁何在，
漫卷诗书喜欲狂。
白日放歌须纵酒，
青春作伴好还乡。
即从巴峡穿巫峡，
便下襄阳向洛阳。

Dufu (712—770)

On Hearing that Imperial Troops Have Recaptured Henan and Hebei

Beyond Jiange quick word has come,
    the northern march set free;
When first I heard, my robes were soaked
    with tears of liberty.

What grief still keeps its sting? —I turn
    to see my family;
In wild delight I bundle up
    my books and poetry.

In broad daylight unchecked I sing,
    and let the wine run free;
My homeland welcomes my return
    in spring's green company.

I'll leave at once, pass by the Gorge
    of Ba, the Gorge of Wu;
To Luoyang City I will fly,
    Xiangyang I'll hurry through.

杜甫(712—770)

江汉

江汉思归客,
乾坤一腐儒。
片云天共远,
永夜月同孤。
落日心犹壮,
秋风病欲疏。
古来存老马,
不必取长途。

Dufu (712—770)

On the River

A homesick traveler upon the river,

Outmoded scholar between earth and sky,

A scrap of cloud adrift on the horizon,

A moon in an eternal night, am I.

But in the setting sun my heart's still ready;

Though Fall gales blow, my illness fades away;

We always find an old horse worth the keeping,

And strength and speed are not the reason why.

岑参(cén shēn)(715—770)

白雪歌送武判官归京 (bái xuě gē sòng wǔ pàn guān guī jīng)

北风卷地白草折,
hú tiān bā yuè jí fēi xuě
胡天八月即飞雪。
忽如一夜春风来,
千树万树梨花开。
散入珠帘湿罗幕,
狐裘不暖锦衾薄。
将军角弓不得控,
都护铁衣冷难着。
瀚海阑干百丈冰,
愁云惨淡万里凝。

Chenshen (715—770)

Song of the White Snow: Farewell to Secretary Wu on His Return to the Capital

The north wind rolls across the earth,
    snapping the white grass stems,
It's August; in the Altai sky,
    a sudden snowstorm comes—
As swiftly as when overnight
    the spring wind starts to blow,
And then ten thousand pear flowers
    in a white-blossomed glow.

The flakes seep through the pearled tent-flap,
    dampen the thick silk screen,
Even fox furs are not so warm,
    brocaded quilts seem thin;
The general may not draw to full
    his frozen bow of horn;
The officers are loath to don
    iron helm and brigandine.

The endless desert's checked and barred
    with furlong waves of ice,
A thousand *li* of gloomy clouds
    freeze in paralysis.

zhōng jūn zhì jiǔ yìn guī kè,
中 军 置 酒 饮 归 客,

hú qín pí pa yǔ qiāng dí
胡 琴 琵 琶 与 羌 笛。

fēn fēn mù xuě xià yuán mén,
纷 纷 暮 雪 下 辕 门,

fēng chè hóng qí dòng bù fān
风 掣 红 旗 冻 不 翻。

lún tái dōng mén sòng jūn qù,
轮 台 东 门 送 君 去,

qù shí xuě mǎn tiān shān lù
去 时 雪 满 天 山 路。

shān huí lù zhuǎn bù jiàn jūn,
山 回 路 转 不 见 君,

xuě shàng kōng liú mǎ xíng chù
雪 上 空 留 马 行 处。

At headquarters there's wine, a feast
   to toast the parting guest

With Altai viol and *Pipa* lute
   and plaintive sweet
Qiang flute;

It's dusk, a heavy snow falls thick
   outside the barracks gate,

Our red flags, tugged by a fierce gale,
   have frozen stiff and straight.

At the east gatehouse of Luntai,
   dear sir, I say farewell:

You go now when the snow is deep
   along the Tianshan trail;

Among the cliff-road's twists and turns
   I have lost sight of you;

In vain the snow records the place
   your horse's hoofprints fell.

张继（约715—约779）

枫桥夜泊

月落乌啼霜满天，
江枫渔火对愁眠。
姑苏城外寒山寺，
夜半钟声到客船。

Zhangji（c 715—c 779）

Nocturne: Lying at Anchor by the Maple Bridge

Moonset. The cawing of a crow.
　Frost glitters through the sky.

Riverbank maples. Fishing lights.
　Sick-hearted, here I lie.

The Hanshan Temple's far outside
　The Suchow city gate;

The temple bell at midnight rings.
　And why is it so late?

刘长卿（约726—789 或790）

逢雪宿芙蓉山主人

日暮苍山远，
天寒白屋贫。
柴门闻犬吠，
风雪夜归人。

Liu Zhangqing (c 726—789 or 790)

Staying on a Night of Wind and Snow with the Host of Hibiscus Mountain

Far teal-blue mountains and the sun's last glow;

In this chill heaven, a poor thatched hut;

You hear a dog bark at the wicker gate—

At night a man comes home in wind and snow.

金昌绪（不详）

春怨

打起黄莺儿，
莫教枝上啼。
啼时惊妾梦，
不得到辽西。

Jin Changxu (Unknown)

Spring Vexation

I've given the yellow warblers a thrashing,

They're not allowed to sing now in our tree;

They've waked your lonely wife while she was dreaming,

So I can't find my way to Fort Liaoxi.

wéi yīng wù
韦应物（约737—791）

chú zhōu xī jiàn
滁州西涧

独怜幽草涧边生，
上有黄鹂深树鸣。
春潮带雨晚来急，
野渡无人舟自横。

Wei Yingwu（c 737—791）

The West Ravine of Chuzhou

My only love's the far-off grass
　　on the ravine's high walls,

Where hidden deep among the trees
　　cry yellow orioles.

The spring flood brings a sudden shower
　　now in the lonely dusk,

And the deserted ferry boat
　　drags crosswise as rain falls.

卢　纶 (739—799)

和张仆射塞下曲·其二

林暗草惊风，

将军夜引弓。

平明寻白羽，

没在石棱中。

Lulun (739—799)

In Reply to Supervisor Zhang Songs of the Frontier (No. 2)

The forest's dark, grass frightened by the wind;

At night the general draws his bow of horn.

They seek the arrow, find it in the dawn

Buried up to the white fletch in the stone.

和张仆射塞下曲·其三

月黑雁飞高,

单于夜遁逃。

欲将轻骑逐,

大雪满弓刀。

In Reply to Supervisor Zhang Songs of the Frontier (No. 3)

The wild geese fly above a moonless sky;

At night the Hun chief's army slips away.

No sooner had our horses gone in pursuit

Than bows and swords with snow were covered high.

李益 (746—829)

江南曲

嫁得瞿塘贾，
朝朝误妾期。
早知潮有信，
嫁与弄潮儿。

Liyi (746—829)

Song to a Melody of the South of Yangtze River

I'm married to the merchant of Gutang,

But everyday he puts off his return.

If I had known the tide keeps its own time,

I would have married a young river-boy.

lǐ kāng chéng bù xiáng
李康成（不详）

cǎi lián qǔ
采莲曲

cǎi lián qù
采莲去，

yuè mò chūn jiāng shǔ
月没春江曙。

cuì diàn hóng xiù shuǐ zhōng yāng
翠钿红袖水中央，

qīng hé lián zǐ zá yī xiāng
青荷莲子杂衣香，

yún qǐ fēng shēng guī lù cháng
云起风生归路长。

guī lù cháng nǎ dé jiǔ
归路长，那得久。

gè huí chuán liǎng yáo shǒu
各回船，两摇手。

Li Kangcheng (Unknown)

Plucking Lotuses: A Song

We're lotus-gathering—
   Moonset and dawn, the river in the spring.

Red sleeves damasked with emeralds
   drift in the middle stream,

The smells of the green lotus buds
   mix with our silks' perfume.

But clouds come up, wind starts to blow,
   it is a long way home,

It's such a long way home,
   can we no longer stay?

As each boat turns to leave,
   It's time to wave goodbye.

孟 郊 (751—814)

洛桥晚望

天津桥下冰初结，
洛阳陌上人行绝。
榆柳萧疏楼阁闲，
月明直见嵩山雪。

Mengjiao (751—814)

Distant View of the Luo Bridge

Beneath the Tianjin Bridge the ice
　　has just begun to show;

In Luoyang City's empty streets
　　no traveler will go;

Willows and elms are bare of leaves,
　　pavilions lie unused;

But in the bright moon brilliantly
　　I see Mount Song's far snow.

孟 郊 (751—814)

游子吟

慈母手中线，

游子身上衣。

临行密密缝，

意恐迟迟归。

谁言寸草心，

报得三春晖。

Mengjiao (751—814)

Song of a Wayfarer

The thread sewn by a mother's loving hand

Now clothes the body of a wandering man.

Before he left she stitched each tiny stitch,

Dreading how long, how long he might be gone.

Ah, one-inch grass blade, can your heart requite

Those three spring months of growth, of splendid light?

韩翃(不详)

寒食

春城无处不飞花,
寒食东风御柳斜。
日暮汉宫传蜡烛,
轻烟散入五侯家。

Hanhong (Unknown)

The Cold Food Festival

Spring in the city; there's nowhere
 the petals do not fly;

Food's eaten cold, the willows of
 the palace bend and sigh.

At sunset, the Han emperor
 passes out candles, though;

And in the Five Dukes' mansions, now,
 light smokes blow thinning by.

wáng jiàn
王　建 (765—830)

yǔ guò shān cūn
雨过山村

雨里鸡鸣一两家，
竹溪村路板桥斜。
妇姑相唤浴蚕去，
闲看中庭栀子花。

Wangjian (765—830)

I Pass Through a Mountain Village in the Rain

A few cocks crow from house to house
　in the unending rain;
A brook, bamboos, a slant plank bridge,
　a winding village lane.
Sisters-in-law call out, to soak
　the silkworms for their cull;
Neglected in the courtyard still
　the gardenia blooms in vain.

王建 (765—830)

望夫石

望夫处,江悠悠。
化为石,不回头。
上头日日风复雨,
行人归来石应语。

Wangjian (765—830)

A Stone, She Gazes After Her Husband

She gazes for her man,
  the river's long and lone;

Her head will never turn:
  she has been changed to stone!

Through rain and wind day after day
  endures the mountain peak;

When that far traveler comes back,
  surely the stone will speak.

张籍（约767—约830）

凉州词·其一

边城暮雨雁飞低,
芦笋初生渐欲齐。
无数铃声遥过碛,
应驮白练到安西。

Zhangji（c 767—c 830）

Song of Liang Zhou（No. 1）

A frontier city; dusk and rain;
　low overhead geese fly.

New shoots of green asparagus
　are all two inches high.

Camel-bells, countless, jangle far
　across moraine and scree;

They should be carrying white silk
　toward our lost Anxi.

张籍（约767—约830）

征妇怨

九月匈奴杀边将，
汉军全没辽水上。
万里无人收白骨，
家家城下招魂葬。
妇人依倚子与夫，
同居贫贱心亦舒。
夫死战场子在腹，
妾身虽存如昼烛。

Zhangji (c 767—c 830)

Lament of the Conscript's Wife

In the ninth month the Hun hordes slew
 the frontier generals;
The armies of the Han all drowned
 where the Liao River rolls.
Nobody in ten thousand *li*
 was left to find their bones;
Families buried dear ones' souls
 beneath the city walls.

A woman leans upon her man
 and on her growing sons;
Our lives together, low and poor,
 were still heart-happy ones.
My son is in my womb, my man
 dead on the field's cold stones;
My body lives, but its light dims—
 a candle's in the sun's.

张籍(约767—约830)

节妇吟·寄东平李司空师道

君知妾有夫,

赠妾双明珠。

感君缠绵意,

系在红罗襦。

妾家高楼连苑起,

良人执戟明光里。

知君用心如日月,

事夫誓拟同生死。

还君明珠双泪垂,

恨不相逢未嫁时。

Zhangji (c 767—c 830)

Song of the Loyal Wife

That I am married, sir, you are aware,

Yet you gave me these two bright pearls to wear;

I sensed your feeling, warm and lingering,

And sewed them to my red silk jacket, there.

But my tall house, its gardens rare,
   are not a paltry thing;

My husband is a halberdier
   for Mingguang's royal king.

For your intentions, they are pure,
   I know, as moon and sun;

But I have sworn to serve my lord
   till death, as we were one.

So I return your pearls, and tears
   roll down both cheeks today;

How bitter that we had not met
   when I was given away!

韩愈(hán yù)(768—824)

听颖师弹琴(tīng yǐng shī tán qín)

昵昵儿女语,
恩怨相尔汝。
划然变轩昂,
勇士赴敌场。
浮云柳絮无根蒂,
天地阔远随飞扬。
喧啾百鸟群,
忽见孤凤凰。
跻攀分寸不可上,
失势一落千丈强。

Hanyu (768—824)

On Hearing Reverend Master Ying Play the *Qin*

A boy and girl who whisper as they woo,

Half-loving, half-aggrieved, it's "you" and "you".

It rises to a grand and martial clang,

A battle-march, with warriors clattering.

Now floating clouds and willow-down

    rootless, drift idly by,

The breeze between vast earth and sky

    blows them, melting, along.

And now it's like a host of chirping birds,

And suddenly a lonely phoenix's song.

It climbs until it can no higher

    for all its venturing,

Then drops at once a thousand feet

    plunging from whence it sprang.

嗟(jiē)余(yú)有(yǒu)两(liǎng)耳(ěr),
未(wèi)省(xǐng)听(tīng)丝(sī)簧(huáng)。
自(zì)闻(wén)颖(yǐng)师(shī)弹(tán),
起(qǐ)坐(zuò)在(zài)一(yī)旁(páng)。
推(tuī)手(shǒu)遽(jù)止(zhǐ)之(zhī),
湿(shī)衣(yī)泪(lèi)滂(pāng)滂(pāng)。
颖(yǐng)乎(hū)尔(ěr)诚(chéng)能(néng),
无(wú)以(yǐ)冰(bīng)炭(tàn)置(zhì)我(wǒ)肠(cháng)!

Alas, though I, unworthy, have two ears,

I knew not how to hear woodwind and string,

But since I've heard the play of Master Ying

I have been restless, cannot sit still long,

Put out my hand to stop the pain-sweet song,

Tears wet my clothes, I feel a sudden pang—

Ah, you are skilled indeed, dear Master Ying:

Do not set fire and ice to burn

   my heart with ravishing!

刘禹锡 (772—842)

乌衣巷

朱雀桥边野草花，
乌衣巷口夕阳斜。
旧时王谢堂前燕，
飞入寻常百姓家。

Liu Yuxi (772—842)

The Lane of the Black Robes

Beside the Scarlet Sparrow Bridge
　wild grass and flowers grow;

Deep into Black Robe Lane the sun
　now setting, slants its glow.

The birds that flocked the noble halls
　of Wang and Xie long past

Fly through the humble dwellings of
　the common people now.

刘禹锡 (772—842)

西塞山怀古

王濬楼船下益州,
金陵王气黯然收。
千寻铁锁沉江底,
一片降幡出石头。
人世几回伤往事,
山形依旧枕寒流。
今逢四海为家日,
故垒萧萧芦荻秋。

Liu Yuxi (772—842)

Xisai Mountain: A Meditation on the Past

When Wang Jun flung his high-decked fleets
   at Yizhou's ancient wall,
The royal *chi* of high Jinling
   darkened, began to pall;
Ten thousand feet of iron chain
   sank to the river-bed,
Processions of surrender-flags
   marked the Stone City's fall.

In human life how often we
   lament old deeds of dread;
Unchanged, the mountain rests upon
   the cold swift river-bend.
Today our home is all that lies
   between the Four Seas spread,
But by the old fort still the reeds
   moan in the autumn wind.

刘禹锡 (772—842)

竹枝词二首·其一

杨柳青青江水平，
闻郎江上唱歌声。
东边日出西边雨，
道是无晴却有晴。

Liu Yuxi (772—842)

Bamboo Frond Song (No. 1)

Within the river-water's glass
    The willow's green is green.
I hear your dear voice by the stream
    Singing a song unseen.
Within the east the sun shines bright,
    But in the west there's rain;
If one face of your weather's dark,
    the other face is fine.

寒 山（不详）

无 题

自乐平生道，
烟萝石洞间。
野情多放旷，
长伴白云闲。
有路不通世，
无心孰可攀。
石床孤夜坐，
圆月上寒山。

Hanshan (Unknown)

Untitled

Free between smoky vines and rocky cave,

A lifelong self-content is all the way.

I feel an open joy in wilderness,

Friend to the white clouds through each lazy day.

Paths there will be that don't lead to this world;

Why climb when heart has no debts left to pay?

All night I sit on a stone bed alone;

Up the Cold Mountain the moon makes its way.

白居易 (772—846)

夜雪

已讶衾枕冷,

复见窗户明。

夜深知雪重,

时闻折竹声。

Bai Juyi (772—846)

Night Snow

The quilt and pillow have got strangely cold;

The window's paper panes begin to glow.

At night I heard how heavy was the snow—

The bamboos, snapped by more than they could hold.

白居易 (772—846)

赋得古原草送别

离离原上草，
一岁一枯荣。
野火烧不尽，
春风吹又生。
远芳侵古道，
晴翠接荒城。
又送王孙去，
萋萋满别情。

Bai Juyi (772—846)

On Parting from a Friend on the Ancient Grasslands

The grass grows thick upon the ancient plain,

Each year a withering and flourishing;

Wildfires may burn it but it flowers again

Never exhausted, in the winds of spring.

Sweeps of sweetgrass invade the ancient way,

Jade in the sun to the abandoned town;

Again I see my young prince ride away

And grief grows thick within me when he's gone.

白居易 (772—846)

钱塘湖春行

孤山寺北贾亭西,
水面初平云脚低。
几处早莺争暖树,
谁家新燕啄春泥。
乱花渐欲迷人眼,
浅草才能没马蹄。
最爱湖东行不足,
绿杨阴里白沙堤。

Bai Juyi (772—846)

Spring Outing at Qiantang Lake

West of Lord Jia's Pavilion,
  north of Lone Mountain Shrine,
The lake's calm face has stilled at last,
  clouds hug the waterline.
The early warblers, here and there,
  pick out the warmest trees,
Spring swallows peck—whose household, where? —
  clay to build colonies.

Soon tumbled flowers will overwhelm
  the dazzled eyes of men;
The new grass scarcely hides the hooves
  of my horse as he moves.
The eastern lakeshore most I love,
  I cannot roam enough
Within the soft green willow-shade
  by the white sandy bluff.

白居易 (772—846)

买花

帝城春欲暮,
喧喧车马度。
共道牡丹时,
相随买花去。
贵贱无常价,
酬直看花数。
灼灼百朵红,
戋戋五束素。
上张幄幕庇,
旁织笆篱护。

Bai Juyi (772—846)

Buying Flowers

Spring's almost over in the capital, and so

Horses and carts go bustling to and fro.

The people cry "Peony time is here!"

Crowd to buy flowers, careless what they owe.

They're cheap or dear, there is no constant price;

If you buy many, then the cost is low;

"Look here, a hundred brightest crimson flowers:

Five bolts of white silk only, fresh to go!"

Above, an awning's spread against the sun,

A wicker fence protects them where they grow;

水洒复泥封，
移来色如故。
家家习为俗，
人人迷不悟。
有一田舍翁，
偶来买花处。
低头独长叹，
此叹无人喻。
一丛深色花，
十户中人赋。

Sprinkled with water, roots packed tight with mud,

The flowers keep their color and their glow.

Each household is accustomed to this now,

Everyone's blinded by obsession though,

Except for one old peasant who sometimes

Comes to buy flowers here, and sees the show:

Alone, he heaves a long sigh, head hung low,

A sigh whose meaning no-one else can know:

One clump of dark-hued flowers costs as much

As land-tax that ten middling households owe!

白居易 (772—846)

卖炭翁

卖炭翁，

伐薪烧炭南山中。

满面尘灰烟火色，

两鬓苍苍十指黑。

卖炭得钱何所营？

身上衣裳口中食。

可怜身上衣正单，

心忧炭贱愿天寒。

Bai Juyi (772—846)

The Old Charcoal-Seller

There is an ancient charcoal-selling man;

He cuts down timber, burns it slow,

High on Mount Zhongnan.

His face ingrained with dust and ash

Is browned with charcoal smoke,

His temples grey with age and toil,

His fingers black as coke.

You sell the charcoal, you get paid,

How do you spend the gains?

To clothe the body's nakedness,

And feed the hunger pains.

Though only thin rags hang upon

His wretched arms and thighs,

He hopes the winter will be cold

So charcoal's price will rise.

夜来城外一尺雪，
晓驾炭车辗冰辙。
牛困人饥日已高，
市南门外泥中歇。
翩翩两骑来是谁？
黄衣使者白衫儿。
手把文书口称敕，
回车叱牛牵向北。
一车炭，
千余斤，
宫使驱将惜不得。
半匹红绡一丈绫，
系向牛头充炭直。

One foot of snow fell overnight,
    He makes an early start;
Down from the hills through rutted ice
He drives the charcoal-cart.

The ox gets tired, the man is starved,
    The sun has risen higher,
He rests outside the Southern Gate
Upon the market mire.

Two horsemen lightly canter up;
    Who are they? By their dress,
One in yellow, one in plain white,
They're couriers, more or less.

With dispatches in hand, they shout
"Imperial command!"
The old man turns his cart, the ox
Drags the whole burden round.

One cart of charcoal's half a ton;
    North to the palace gate
The envoys chivvy him, and now
He must unload the weight.

In grief he's paid but half a bolt
Of muslin, dyed cheap red,
And but nine feet of low-grade silk
Flung round the ox's head.

李 绅 (772—846)

悯农二首·其一

春种一粒粟，

秋收万颗子。

四海无闲田，

农夫犹饿死。

Linshen (772—846)

A Pair of Ancient Ballads Sympathy for the Peasants (No.1)

In spring you plant just one small millet-seed,

In autumn reap ten thousand ears of grain;

Between the Four Seas lies no idle land,

Yet still the farmer starves to death in pain.

悯农二首·其二

锄禾日当午，

汗滴禾下土。

谁知盘中餐，

粒粒皆辛苦？

A Pair of Ancient Ballads Sympathy for the Peasants(No.2)

    Beneath the noonday sun he hoes up weeds,

    His sweat falls earthwards to the crop it feeds;

    Know, you who think a meal comes on a plate,

    The hot and bitter toil that each grain needs!

崔护 (772—846)

题都城南庄

去年今日此门中，
人面桃花相映红。
人面不知何处去，
桃花依旧笑春风。

Cuihu (772—846)

Inscribed on a Door in the South Neighborhood of the Capital

Within this very entrance hall today one year ago
The pink peach blossoms and her face gave back each other's glow.
I do not know where is the place where that soft face has gone;
But the peach blooms remain, and still smile when the spring winds blow.

柳宗元（773—819）

登柳州城楼寄漳汀封连四州

城上高楼接大荒，
海天愁思正茫茫。
惊风乱飐芙蓉水，
密雨斜侵薜荔墙。
岭树重遮千里目，
江流曲似九回肠。
共来百越文身地，
犹自音书滞一乡。

Liu Zongyuan (773—819)

Ascending the Barbican of Liuzhou for the Four Governors of Zhangzhou, Tingzhou, Fengzhou, and Lianzhou

    The great tower on the city wall
        adjoins a vast wide land;
Huge sea-and-sky thoughts trouble me,
        so hard to understand.
A sudden gust of wind disturbs
        the lotus in the pool;
Thick rain slants down, invades the fig
        where on the wall it's trained.
A thousand *li* the layers of trees
        hinder the yearning eye,
The River Liu's far loopings bend
        as grief's nine heartstrings wind;
Amid a hundred tribes' tattoos
        together we're exiled,
But messages are late and slow
        here in this foreign land.

柳宗元(liǔ zōng yuán) (773—819)

渔翁(yú wēng)

渔翁(yú wēng)夜(yè)傍(bàng)西(xī)岩(yán)宿(sù),
晓(xiǎo)汲(jí)清(qīng)湘(xiāng)燃(rán)楚(chǔ)竹(zhú)。
烟(yān)销(xiāo)日(rì)出(chū)不(bù)见(jiàn)人(rén),
欸(ǎi)乃(nǎi)一(yī)声(shēng)山(shān)水(shuǐ)绿(lǜ)。
回(huí)看(kàn)天(tiān)际(jì)下(xià)中(zhōng)流(liú),
岩(yán)上(shàng)无(wú)心(xīn)云(yún)相(xiāng)逐(zhú)。

Liu Zongyuan (773—819)

The Old Fisherman

At night beside the western cliff

    he sleeps in his lean-to;

At dawn he drinks the bright clear Xiang,

    burns the bamboos of Chu.

The smoke is gone, the sun comes out,

    by now he is unseen:

Only the creaking of an oar

    in crags and waters green.

Far down the middle reaches he

    turns back and sees the view,

Empty of mind, above the cliffs,

    the idle clouds pursue.

柳宗元 (773—819)

江雪

千山鸟飞绝，

万径人踪灭。

孤舟蓑笠翁，

独钓寒江雪。

Liu Zongyuan (773—819)

Snow River

Birds fly no more among these thousand hills,

Men's footprints blank along ten thousand ways:

With boat, straw hat and cape one old man stays

Fishing alone in the snow-river's chills.

元稹 (779—831)

行宫

寥落古行宫，
宫花寂寞红。
白头宫女在，
闲坐说玄宗。

Yuanzhen (779—831)

The Country Palace

The old imperial lodge is bare and worn;

The palace garden's flowers bloom forlorn.

The last court ladies idle, tresses white,

Murmur the name of Xuan Zong, Heaven-born.

贾 岛 (779—843)

剑 客

十年磨一剑，
霜刃未曾试。
今日把示君，
谁有不平事？

Jiadao (779—843)

The Gentle Swordsman

For ten years I have honed this single sword;

Its ice-bright blade has never yet been tried.

Today I draw and show it to you, lord;

Are there injustices unrectified?

贾岛 (779—843)

寻隐者不遇

松下问童子，
言师采药去。
只在此山中，
云深不知处。

Jiadao (779—843)

I Visit the Hermit, but He Is Not There

I ask the boy beneath the dark green pine;

The master's gathering herbs, he would suppose.

Where? On the mountain somewhere.

And which way?

—Deep in the clouds, but where, nobody knows.

李 贺 (790—816)

南园·其一

花枝草蔓眼中开,
小白长红越女腮。
可怜日暮嫣香落,
嫁与春风不用媒。

Lihe (790—816)

Southern Garden (No. 1)

Blossoming branches, trailing flowers
    open within my eye;
The paler white and richer rose
    blush like the girls of Yueh.
At evening, lovely, pitiful,
    the fragrant petals fall;
Wed to the winds of spring, they need
    no matchmaker at all.

李贺 (790—816)

金铜仙人辞汉歌

茂陵刘郎秋风客,
夜闻马嘶晓无迹。
画栏桂树悬秋香,
三十六宫土花碧。
魏官牵车指千里,
东关酸风射眸子。
空将汉月出宫门,
忆君清泪如铅水。
衰兰送客咸阳道,
天若有情天亦老。
携盘独出月荒凉,
渭城已远波声小。

Lihe (790—816)

The Copper-Gold God's Farewell to the Realm of Han: Song

That Liu in the Mao Tomb is but
    a guest in the fall wind;
At night one hears his horses neigh,
    at dawn no trace is seen.
Sweet laurel fragrance hangs between
    autumnal carving columns,
Thirty-six palaces now lie
    under the mosses green.

"Wei guards set out to drag my wain
    wellnigh a thousand *li*,
The dart-like gale of the East Pass
    pierced my eye cruelly.
Only the Han moon by the gate
    remained to bid farewell;
Bright tears of molten lead, my lord,
    recall your memory."
And drooping orchids said goodbye
    beside the Xianyan Way,
If Heaven itself can feel at all,
    Heaven must age, as we.
He took his dew-dish out alone
    beneath the moon-bleak sky;
The town of Wei is far away,
    silent its waters' sigh.

李 贺 (790—816)

雁门太守行

黑云压城城欲摧,
甲光向日金鳞开。
角声满天秋色里,
塞上燕脂凝夜紫。
半卷红旗临易水,
霜重鼓寒声不起。
报君黄金台上意,
提携玉龙为君死!

Lihe (790—816)

Song: the Commander of Wild Goose Gate

Black clouds crush down the city wall,
    the city soon shall fall,
But suddenly the sun's bright face
    flashes on armor scale;
The sky is full of ringing horns
    in the autumnal light,
About the fortress blood like rouge
    clots purple in the night.

Red banners, furled, now march against
    the fatal river Yi,
So bitter is the frost, the drum
    beats dully and heavily.
On the Gold Platform those kind gifts
    given me by my lord
I shall repay, although I die,
    with my Jade Dragon sword.

李贺 (790—816)

老夫采玉歌

采玉采玉须水碧，
琢作步摇徒好色。
老夫饥寒龙为愁，
蓝溪水气无清白。
夜雨冈头食蓁子，
杜鹃口血老夫泪。
蓝溪之水厌生人，
身死千年恨溪水。
斜山柏风雨如啸，
泉脚挂绳青袅袅。
村寒白屋念娇婴，
古台石磴悬肠草。

Lihe (790—816)

Song of the Old Jade Miner

Dig the jade, dig the jade,
    the emerald-water hue;
Carved for a pendant it will serve
    a pretty lady's glow.
A little man, starving and cold,
    creek-dragons pity me,
The Blue Creek waters roil and cloud
    and lose their clarity.

Upon the clifftop, in night rain,
    on hazelnuts I dine;
It's said the cuckoo's beak sings blood,
    as this poor man weeps now;
The Blue Creek hates the strangers who
    disturb its waters' flow;
And when my body's dead, my soul
    will hate these waters too.

Howling through crags and cypresses
    the gusty raindrops blow,
Upon a swinging rope I hang,
    the green spring far below.
My white hut's in the village cold;
    I miss my babies dear;
On old stepped terraces of stone
    grows grass called "fatherwoe".

李贺 (790—816)

李凭箜篌引

吴丝蜀桐张高秋,

空山凝云颓不流。

江娥啼竹素女愁,

李凭中国弹箜篌。

昆山玉碎凤凰叫,

芙蓉泣露香兰笑。

十二门前融冷光,

二十三丝动紫皇。

Lihe (791—816)

Upon the Sounds of Li Ping's *Konghou*: Yin

Wu silk, Shu polished wood resound
   into the high fall sky,
The empty mountain, curdled clouds,
   becalmed by their sad cry.
The nymph's tears speckle the bamboos,
   White Goddess sighs with woe,
For Li Ping plays his great Konghou
   in the capital city of Tang.

The shattering of Mount Kun jade,
   the phoenix's wild scream,
The weeping of the lotus-dew,
   sweet orchids' laughing dream.
The cold light by the twelve great gates
   melts in the music's thaw,
Twenty-three silken strings vibrate
   the Purple Emperor.

nǚ wā liàn shí bǔ tiān chù,
女 娲 炼 石 补 天 处,

shí pò tiān jīng dòu qiū yǔ。
石 破 天 惊 逗 秋 雨。

mèng rù shén shān jiāo shén yù,
梦 入 神 山 教 神 妪,

lǎo yú tiào bō shòu jiāo wǔ。
老 鱼 跳 波 瘦 蛟 舞。

wú zhì bù mián yǐ guì shù,
吴 质 不 眠 倚 桂 树,

lù jiǎo xié fēi shī hán tù。
露 脚 斜 飞 湿 寒 兔。

The goddess Nüwa melted stone

    to mend the war-torn sky,

The sky, shocked by the breaking stone,

    stirs the fall rain to fly.

The dreamsong threads god-mountain caves,

    makes the old witches gay,

The old fishes leap the waves,

    dancing flood-dragons play.

When Wuzhi could not sleep, he leaned

    on the sweet laurel tree;

The dewdrops fly aslant upon

    Moon-rabbit's chill wet ray.

李 贺 (790—816)

梦 天

老兔寒蟾泣天色，
云楼半开壁斜白。
玉轮轧露湿团光，
鸾珮相逢桂香陌。
黄尘清水三山下，
更变千年如走马。
遥望齐州九点烟，
一泓海水杯中泻。

Lihe (791—816)

Dream Sky

A rabbit old, a toad of cold

Weep heaven-colored tears;

Across the cloud-tower's opening door

A slant of white appears.

The jade wheel crushes out the dew,

Soaking its ring of light,

Jade-Phoenix meets me on the way,

Sweet laurel scents the night.

Beneath the Three Peaks land and sea

Exchange, transmogrify;

A thousand turning years flit past

As horses gallop by;

I gaze at China, its nine realms

But points of smoke sent up,

The sea is but a puddle spilled

Out of a water-cup.

朱庆馀 (797—?)

近试上张水部

洞房昨夜停红烛，
待晓堂前拜舅姑。
妆罢低声问夫婿，
画眉深浅入时无。

Zhu Qingyu (797—?)

Presented to Mr. Zhang of the Water Ministry on the Eve of My Examination

The bridal chamber glowed last night
　with the red candle's seal;
I wait to greet new parents soon
　at dawn in the great hall.
Dressed and made up, I whisper now:
　"Lord husband, do you feel
My brows are brushed too black, or not,
　to suit the present style?"

杜牧（803—852）

泊秦淮

烟笼寒水月笼沙，
夜泊秦淮近酒家。
商女不知亡国恨，
隔江犹唱后庭花。

Dumu（803—852）

Moored by the Qinhuai River

Mist clothes the chilly water as
　　the moonlight clothes the sand；
My boat's tied up on the Qinhuai,
　　the wineshops close at hand.
The singer-girls have not a care
　　lest their homeland should fall；
Across the river still they sing
　　"The Flower Behind the Hall."

杜牧(803—852)

江南春

千里莺啼绿映红,
水村山郭酒旗风。
南朝四百八十寺,
多少楼台烟雨中。

Dumu(803—852)

Spring in the South of Yangtze River

A thousand *li* the warblers sing,
　　green-crimson symmetries;
Brook-hamlets, hilltop city walls,
　　wine-banners in the breeze.
The Southern Dynasty held once
　　four hundred and eighty shrines;
How many tall pagodas stood
　　amid the mists and rains!

杜牧 (803—852)

山行

远上寒山石径斜，
白云生处有人家。
停车坐爱枫林晚，
霜叶红于二月花。

Dumu (803—852)

Mountain Journey

I took the winding rocky path
    High in the mountain chill;
The white clouds deepened, but there were
    Some human homesteads still;
I stopped my wagon, for I love
    Late maple groves in fall,
Whose frost-struck leaves are redder than
    The spring flowers' festival.

杜牧 (803—852)

赠别·其二

多情却似总无情，
唯觉樽前笑不成。
蜡烛有心还惜别，
替人垂泪到天明。

Dumu (803—852)

Parting Gift (No.2)

As always, I feel much but can show nothing,

I feel I cannot smile over the wine;

The candle's heart, its wick, grieves for our parting,

And wax tears flow till dawn in place of mine.

杜牧 (803—852)

秋夕

银烛秋光冷画屏，
轻罗小扇扑流萤。
天阶夜色凉如水，
坐看牵牛织女星。

Dumu (803—852)

Autumn Night

Upon a painted screen a candle throws
    A cold autumnal glow;
She flaps a tiny fan of fragile silk
    Against the fireflies' flow;
The dim stairs under the night sky are chill
    As water where she lies;
Two stars, the Cowherd and the Weaver-Girl,
    Shine, parted, in her eyes.

李涉(不详)
lǐ shè bù xiáng

牧童词
mù tóng cí

朝牧牛，
zhāo mù niú,

牧牛下江曲。
mù niú xià jiāng qū.

夜牧牛，
yè mù niú,

牧牛度村谷。
mù niú dù cūn gǔ.

荷蓑出林春雨细，
hè suō chū lín chūn yǔ xì,

芦管卧吹莎草绿。
lú guǎn wò chuī suō cǎo lǜ.

乱插蓬蒿箭满腰，
luàn chā péng hāo jiàn mǎn yāo,

不怕猛虎欺黄犊。
bù pà měng hǔ qī huáng dú.

Lishe (Unknown)

Song of the Boy Cowherd

At dawn he drives his cow,

He drives his cow down to the river-bow.

At night he drives his cow

Home to the village in the deep vale's brow.

In his straw rain-cape, from the woods

   he wends in thin spring rain;

Lying on green grass in the sand

   his flute he starts to blow.

He's stuck his "arrows"—fleabane stalks—

   into his belt, so now

He doesn't fear the tiger fierce

   who'd scare his yellow cow.

皎然(不详)

闻钟

古寺寒山上,
远钟扬好风。
声余月树动,
响尽霜天空。
永夜一禅子,
泠然心境中。

Jiaoran (Unknown)

Hearing a Bell (on Cold Mountain)

From the old shrine on Hanshan comes a clang,

A far bell like the sweet wind's spreading song.

The Moon-Tree rings with its long lingering,

The frosty sky is emptied by its gong.

Long through the night the seeker after Zen

Lets the mind chill, and still, and hang.

wēn tíng yún
温庭筠（约 812—866）

shāng shān zǎo xíng
商山早行

chén qǐ dòng zhēng duó
晨 起 动 征 铎，

kè xíng bēi gù xiāng
客 行 悲 故 乡。

jī shēng máo diàn yuè
鸡 声 茅 店 月，

rén jì bǎn qiáo shuāng
人 迹 板 桥 霜。

hú yè luò shān lù
槲 叶 落 山 路，

zhǐ huā míng yì qiáng
枳 花 明 驿 墙。

yīn sī dù líng mèng
因 思 杜 陵 梦，

fú yàn mǎn huí táng
凫 雁 满 回 塘。

Wen Tingyun (c 812—866)

Early Departure on Mount Shang

At dawn we rise to go, the horse-bells chime,

The traveler pining for his native home.

Cockcrow; the deep-thatched guest house; the pale moon;

Footprints in the plank bridge's frosty rime.

Oak leaves are falling on the mountain trail,

On the Post's wall bright orange-blossoms climb;

The Du Tomb that I dreamed of comes to mind:

Its pond is full of wild geese, just come home.

温庭筠（约 812—866）

赠少年

江海相逢客恨多，
秋风叶下洞庭波。
酒酣夜别淮阴市，
月照高楼一曲歌。

Wen Tingyun (c 812—866)

For a Young Man

We met by chance while voyaging,
　both homesick, both alone;
Beneath the windblown autumn leaves,
　where Dongting's waves roll in.
Tonight let's drink, bid farewell at
　the market of Huaiyin;
The moon gleams on the tall-decked tower—
　Let's sing one last song then!

李商隐（约813—约858）

嫦娥

云母屏风烛影深，
长河渐落晓星沉。
嫦娥应悔偷灵药，
碧海青天夜夜心。

Li Shangyin (c 813—c 858)

The Moon Goddess Chang'e

A mica screen; a candle throws
　　long shadows on the wall;

The heavenly river slides; dawn comes,
　　and now the last stars fall.

Chang'e should regret now that she stole
　　the elixir of life;

Night after night with restless heart:
　　jade sea, blue sky is all.

李商隐(约813—约858)

无题

昨夜星辰昨夜风,
画楼西畔桂堂东。
身无彩凤双飞翼,
心有灵犀一点通。
隔座送钩春酒暖,
分曹射覆蜡灯红。
嗟余听鼓应官去,
走马兰台类转蓬。

Li Shangyin (c 813—c 858)

Untitled

Last night it was all wind and star,

    last night was wind and star;

Eastward there was the Laurel Hall,

    westward the Painted Tower.

Though we're not tinted phoenixes

    fledged with each other's wings,

Our hearts are of the magic horn,

    joined at its secret core.

Sending hooks across seats,

    drinking the warm sweet wine,

Divided, played the Guessing Game,

    at the red candle hour;

Sighing I hear the dawn drum call

    me to the hall of State,

Swept off on horseback as the wind

    sweeps leaves for evermore.

李商隐（约813—约858）

锦瑟

锦瑟无端五十弦，
一弦一柱思华年。
庄生晓梦迷蝴蝶，
望帝春心托杜鹃。
沧海月明珠有泪，
蓝田日暖玉生烟。
此情可待成追忆，
只是当时已惘然。

Li Shangyin (c 813—c 858)

The Inlaid Zither

Why should this inlaid zither have

   just fifty silken strings?

Each string, each fret reminds me of

   one year of my flowerings.

Young Zhuang woke from his dream confused:

   was he a butterfly?

Lord Wang in spring gave his heart to

   a cuckoo's murmurings.

The bright moon on the azure sea

   stirs tears in the pearl,

The warm sun on the Blue Stone Field

   engenders smoke from jade:

How could these feelings, then, become

   enduring memory,

Which, at the time, were full, themselves,

   of disappointment's shade?

李商隐(约813—约858)

隋宫

紫泉宫殿锁烟霞,
欲取芜城作帝家。
玉玺不缘归日角,
锦帆应是到天涯。
于今腐草无萤火,
终古垂杨有暮鸦。
地下若逢陈后主,
岂宜重问后庭花。

Li Shangyin (c 813—c 858)

The Palace of the Sui Emperor

The palace by the Purple Spring

   is swathed in rose smoke-pall.

You'd take a city laid to waste

   to be your capital.

But the Jade Seal, not meant for you,

   came to a sun-born brow;

You'd hoped your brocade sails would reach

   the far shores of it all.

Since you, no fireflies breed within

   the dying grass of fall;

But the drooped poplar trees at dusk

   still mark the crows' old call.

If in the underworld you find

   House Chen's last emperor,

Would it be meet to ask about

   "The Flower behind the Hall"?

李商隐 (约813—约858)

夜雨寄北

君问归期未有期,
巴山夜雨涨秋池。
何当共剪西窗烛,
却话巴山夜雨时。

Li Shangyin (c 813—c 858)

A Letter to the North Written on a Rainy Night

You ask me when I will return,
　　return I can't say when;
Here in the Sichuan mountains, night
　　swells the fall ponds with rain.
When, by our western window, shall
　　we trim the candle flame,
Remember that dark mountain night
　　and the fall rain again?

李商隐（约813—约858）

乐游原

向晚意不适，
驱车登古原。
夕阳无限好，
只是近黄昏。

Li Shangyin (c 813—c 858)

Leyou Plateau

As evening fell, in some disquiet of spirit,

I drove my wagon up on the high plain.

The sunset's loveliness was infinite,

But yellow dusk was coming all too soon.

李商隐(约813—约858)

晚晴

深居俯夹城,
春去夏犹清。
天意怜幽草,
人间重晚晴。
并添高阁迥,
微注小窗明。
越鸟巢干后,
归飞体更轻。

Li Shangyin (c 813—c 858)

A Fine Evening

I'm snug above the passage with high walls on both sides,

Though spring is gone, my summer still shines clear;

Heaven yet blesses the secluded grasses,

It is the golden evening men hold dear.

And from my high pavilion I see far;

Mild light pours through my little window here;

The Yue birds' nests are dry now; they fly home,

Their bodies lighter in this clear bright air.

黄巢（820—884）

题菊花

飒飒西风满院栽,
蕊寒香冷蝶难来。
他年我若为青帝,
报与桃花一处开。

Huangchao (820—884)

Ode to the Chrysanthemums

The west wind rustles in the yard
   that's thick with your full flower,
But chill your stamens, cold your scent;
   no butterflies fly here.
If in another year I were
   Spring's great green emperor,
I'd grant you, with the noble peach,
   to bloom the selfsame hour.

韦庄 (约836—910)

台城

江雨霏霏江草齐，
六朝如梦鸟空啼。
无情最是台城柳，
依旧烟笼十里堤。

Weizhuang (c 836—910)

Tai City

It rains and rains upon the river,
　　the grass grows thick and high;
Six dynasties have fled like dreams,
　　the birds inanely cry.
How utterly indifferent are
　　the willows in the city,
Shrouded in mist for these ten *li*,
　　as the low dike goes by.

聂夷中 (niè yí zhōng) (837—884)

咏田家 (yǒng tián jiā)

二月卖新丝，
五月粜新谷。
医得眼前疮，
剜却心头肉。
我愿君王心，
化作光明烛。
不照绮罗筵，
只照逃亡屋。

Nie Yizhong (837—884)

Lament of the Peasant Family

By February they've sold the raw cocoons,

By May they've sold the seed crop of the grain;

As if to heal a sore upon the skin

They'd cut flesh from the heart and graft it in.

I hope the heart of our high emperor

Will turn into a candle warm and bright—

Not in a banquet's fancy chandelier,

But for abandoned farms the one true light.

皮日休（约838—约883）

汴河怀古·其二

尽道隋亡为此河，
至今千里赖通波。
若无水殿龙舟事，
共禹论功不较多。

Pi Rixiu (c 838—c 883)

The Bian River Reach of the Grand Canal: A Meditation (No. 2)

Everyone says the House of Sui
　　fell with this waterway,
Yet ever since, we have relied
　　on its good thousand *li*.
Without the floating palaces
　　and dragon barges, he
Might not fall short of great Yu's fame
　　and be revered today.

杜荀鹤(846—904)

山中寡妇

夫因兵死守蓬茅，
麻苎衣衫鬓发焦。
桑柘废来犹纳税，
田园荒后尚征苗。
时挑野菜和根煮，
旋斫生柴带叶烧。
任是深山更深处，
也应无计避征徭。

Du Xunhe (846—904)

The Widow in the Mountains

Her husband died in war; she keeps

    their thatched house on her own.

Sackcloth and burlap are her clothes,

    her hair is dull and wan.

The silkworm mulberries lie waste,

    yet levies must be paid;

The field and garden run to seed

    but the grain-tax goes on.

Now often she must pluck wild herbs

    to thicken her weak gruel,

Hack up fresh sticks still green with leaves

    to feed her fire—alone.

Deep in the deepest mountain-vale

    there is no trick to fool

Or stave off the corvée's harsh weight

    and land-tax hard as stone!

杜荀鹤(846—904)

送人游吴

君到姑苏见，
人家尽枕河。
古宫闲地少，
水港小桥多。
夜市卖菱藕，
春船载绮罗。
遥知未眠月，
乡思在渔歌。

Du Xunhe (846—904)

Farewell to a Friend on His Departure for the Land of Wu

In Suzhou, sir, here's what will greet your eyes:

The homes all nestled on the riverside,

The ancient palaces, scant open space,

A crowd of docks, small bridges far and wide.

At night they're selling *ling* and lotus root;

"Spring-boats" are gay with gauze and silken braid.

Though far, I'll know the moon won't let you sleep,

Homesick, with fishing songs on every side.

秦韬玉（不详）

贫女

蓬门未识绮罗香，
拟托良媒益自伤。
谁爱风流高格调，
共怜时世俭梳妆。
敢将十指夸针巧，
不把双眉斗画长。
苦恨年年压金线，
为他人作嫁衣裳。

Qin Taoyu (Unknown)

Poor Girl

A wicker door has barred me from

    the fragrant silk brocade;

I seek a clever matchmaker

    but am a poor sad maid.

Who is there, tasteful and refined,

    keeping a lofty style,

Who will with me enjoy the years

    frugally well-arrayed?

I dare praise my ten fingers' skill

    with needle, yarn, and lisle;

I do not draw my eyebrows long,

    compete with paint and shade.

But year by year in grief I press

    the gold thread into braid

On skirts and bodices that are

    for others' weddings made!

第二部分 宋诗

林逋 (967—1028)

山园小梅二首·其一

众芳摇落独暄妍,
占尽风情向小园。
疏影横斜水清浅,
暗香浮动月黄昏。

霜禽欲下先偷眼,
粉蝶如知合断魂。
幸有微吟可相狎,
不须檀板共金樽。

Linbu (967—1028)

Plum Blossoms in the Mountain Garden (No.1)

The flowers fade in this cold wind,
   the plum blooms here alone,
And gives this little garden here
   a brightness of its own;
Sparse shadows slant into the pond
   clear in its shallow light;
Beneath the evening moon there drifts
   a soft scent of delight.

When the chilled swallow spies these blooms,
   it makes the plum its goal;
If butterflies could know their bliss,
   They'd lose their mind and soul;
How lucky I, to murmur words
   of gentle poetry,
Who needs the golden cup, the clack
   of song and jollity?

范仲淹 (989—1052)

江上渔者

江上往来人，
但爱鲈鱼美。
君看一叶舟，
出没风波里。

Fan Zhongyan (989—1052)

Fisherman upon the River

Upon the river people come and go,

The sweet perch-flesh the only thing they crave.

See that boat, sir, like a tiny leaf,

Rising and sinking in the wind and wave.

梅尧臣 (1002—1060)

陶者

陶尽门前土,

屋上无片瓦。

十指不沾泥,

鳞鳞居大厦。

Mei Yaochen (1002—1060)

The Potter's Song

The clay around his house he's turned to pots,

His own roof doesn't bear a single tile.

There's no mud on the mansion-dweller's hands,

But still it's fully scaled with handmade tiles.

王安石（1021—1086）

登飞来峰

飞来山上千寻塔，
闻说鸡鸣见日升。
不畏浮云遮望眼，
自缘身在最高层。

Wang Anshi (1021—1086)

Ascending Feilai Peak

On Feilai Peak there rises up
    an even taller tower;
There, when the first cock crows, you'll see
    the first ray of the sun.
I do not fear those layers of cloud
    that shroud my distant view;
For here I stand on Feilai Peak,
    my mind high, wide, and one.

王安石 (1021—1086)

梅花

墙角数枝梅，
凌寒独自开。
遥知不是雪，
为有暗香来。

Wang Anshi (1021—1086)

Wintersweet

The wintersweet plum branches by the wall

Bloom in the corner heedless of the cold.

Even from far you'd not take them for snow,

For their soft scent, unseen, will let you know.

王安石 (1021—1086)

泊船瓜洲

京口瓜洲一水间,
钟山只隔数重山。
春风又绿江南岸,
明月何时照我还。

Wang Anshi (1021—1086)

Mooring at Guazhou

Only one river separates
    Jingkou now from Guazhou,
A few green hills are all that stand
    between us and Zhongshan.
On the great river's southern bank
    Spring wind again will blow;
So when shall I go home at last
    beneath the shining moon?

王安石（1021—1086）

元日

爆竹声中一岁除，
春风送暖入屠苏。
千门万户曈曈日，
总把新桃换旧符。

Wang Anshi（1021—1086）

Lunar New Year's Day

The crackle of firecrackers ends
   the old year that's now gone;
People out in the warm spring wind
   drink the newly brewed Tusu wine.
Upon a thousand homes the sun
   shines in its first fresh dawn;
They take down the old peachwood charms,
   put up new ones again.

程颢 (1032—1085)

春日偶成

云淡风轻近午天，
傍花随柳过前川。
时人不识余心乐，
将谓偷闲学少年。

Chenghao (1032—1085)

Impromptu Lines on a Spring Day

The clouds are thin, the breeze is mild
　　near noon on this spring day;
I brush the willows and the flowers
　　along the riverside.
People can't know my inner happiness,
　　the secret hidden joy,
They think I learned from truant boys
　　how to just let things slide.

苏轼 (1037—1101)

题西林壁

横看成岭侧成峰,
远近高低各不同。
不识庐山真面目,
只缘身在此山中。

Sushi (1037—1101)

Inscribed on a Temple Wall

Face-on, a whole range meets the eye;
　Side-on, one peak stands clear.
From near or far, or low or high,
　It's different everywhere.

I cannot know Mount Lu's true face,
　And here's the reason why:
I am myself part of this place,
　Within its rock and sky.

苏轼 (1037—1101)

惠崇春江晚景

竹外桃花三两枝,
春江水暖鸭先知。
蒌蒿满地芦芽短,
正是河豚欲上时。

Sushi (1037—1101)

Hui Chong's River Scenes on a Spring Evening

Two or three peach blossoms
    are blooming outside the bamboo forest,
The ducks are the first to feel
    the water warmth when spring comes.
The lush wormwood covers the bank,
    the reed buds now appear,
And spawning pufferfish ascend
    along the flooding streams.

苏 轼 (1037—1101)

惠州一绝

罗浮山下四时春，
卢橘杨梅次第新。
日啖荔枝三百颗，
不辞长作岭南人。

Sushi (1037—1101)

Glorious Huizhou

Under the heights of Mount Luofu
　　It's spring through all the year,
The loquats and the bayberry
　　fresh ripening in turn;
If I could eat three hundred of
　　these lychees every day,
I think I'd be a Lingnan man
　　and settle down and stay.

苏轼 (1037—1101)

饮湖上初晴后雨

水光潋滟晴方好，
山色空蒙雨亦奇。
欲把西湖比西子，
淡妆浓抹总相宜。

Sushi (1037—1101)

Drinking on the Lake: First Shine, Then Rain

The water-light upon the waves
    in sunshine is quite fine;
The misty mountain-tints beneath the rain
    have magic of their own.
I'd liken West Lake's beauty to
    that of the famed Xi Shi:
Whether untouched or painted, none
    were lovelier than she.

李清照 (1084—1155)

夏日绝句

生当作人杰,
死亦为鬼雄。
至今思项羽,
不肯过江东。

Li Qingzhao (1084—1155)

Quatrain for a Summer Day

Live as a hero when you are alive,

Be a great ghost when you must come to die.

Think of Xiang Yu, he who disdained to flee

Back to Jiangdong that day gone by.

陆游 (1125—1210)

冬夜读书示子聿

古人学问无遗力，
少壮工夫老始成。
纸上得来终觉浅，
绝知此事要躬行。

Luyou (1125—1210)

Teaching Ziyu to Read on a Winter's Night

The ancients spared no pains to learn,
　　and learning, yes, is hard,
The skills you learn when you are young
　　will ripen in old age.
And paper-knowledge by itself
　　is shallow in the end;
Surely if you would know the truth,
　　bow to the task of sage.

陆游(lù yóu)(1125—1210)

游山西村(yóu shān xī cūn)

莫(mò)笑(xiào)农(nóng)家(jiā)腊(là)酒(jiǔ)浑(hún),

丰(fēng)年(nián)留(liú)客(kè)足(zú)鸡(jī)豚(tún)。

山(shān)重(chóng)水(shuǐ)复(fù)疑(yí)无(wú)路(lù),

柳(liǔ)暗(àn)花(huā)明(míng)又(yòu)一(yī)村(cūn)。

箫(xiāo)鼓(gǔ)追(zhuī)随(suí)春(chūn)社(shè)近(jìn),

衣(yī)冠(guān)简(jiǎn)朴(pǔ)古(gǔ)风(fēng)存(cún)。

从(cóng)今(jīn)若(ruò)许(xǔ)闲(xián)乘(chéng)月(yuè),

拄(zhǔ)杖(zhàng)无(wú)时(shí)夜(yè)叩(kòu)门(mén)。

Luyou (1125—1210)

Visiting the Village to the West of Sanshan Township

Don't scorn the farmers' murky wine,
　　homebrewed in the twelfth lunar month.
At harvest, you are richly served
　　a fish and chicken feast.
Stacked ridges and branched torrents seem
　　to offer no way through,
Then bright with hidden willows, flowers,
　　a village is released.

Spring celebrations, flute and drum
　　follow the season soon,
In rustic hats and smocks the past
　　renews its finery;
If some night I have time to take
　　advantage of the moon,
I'll knock your door with my old stick,
　　Just as it used to be.

范成大 (1126—1193)

四时田园杂兴·其二十五

梅子金黄杏子肥,

麦花雪白菜花稀。

日长篱落无人过,

惟有蜻蜓蛱蝶飞。

Fan Chengda (1126—1193)

Garden Poems of the Four Seasons (No. 25)

The plums turn gold, the apricots
　　put on a fleshy glow,
Some yellow rapeseed flowers among
　　thick wheat-bloom white as snow.
The day is getting on, nobody comes
　　along the fence today,
But for a passing dragonfly,
　　a butterfly or two.

fàn chéng dà
范成大（1126—1193）

四时田园杂兴·其三十一
sì shí tián yuán zá xīng · qí sān shí yī

昼出耘田夜绩麻，
zhòu chū yún tián yè jì má

村庄儿女各当家。
cūn zhuāng ér nǚ gè dāng jiā

童孙未解供耕织，
tóng sūn wèi jiě gòng gēng zhī

也傍桑阴学种瓜。
yě bàng sāng yīn xué zhòng guā

Fan Chengda（1126—1193）

Garden Poems of the Four Seasons（No. 31）

By day they weed the fields, by night
　rub hemp to make up string,
They take care of their families
　and manage everything.
The children, who can't plow the soil
　or weave yet properly,
Sow melon seeds beneath the shade
　of the green mulberry.

杨万里 (1127—1206)

小池

泉眼无声惜细流，
树阴照水爱晴柔。
小荷才露尖尖角，
早有蜻蜓立上头。

Yang Wanli (1127—1206)

A Little Pond

The silent trickle of this spring
    enjoys its soft outflow;
In the tree-shade the water loves
    to mirror the bright scene.
No sooner does the lotus show
    its bud-tip to the sky
Than it is occupied at once
    by a quick dragonfly.

朱熹 (1130—1200)

观书有感·其一

半亩方塘一鉴开，
天光云影共徘徊。
问渠那得清如许？
为有源头活水来。

Zhuxi (1130—1200)

Reflections on Reading Books (No.1)

A pond just over three ares across
    reflects the whole bright sky,
The sky-light and the shadowed clouds
    together wander by.
I ask myself how it can stay
    so luminous and clear?
Because there's an unceasing source
    of living water here.

朱熹 (zhū xī) (1130—1200)

偶成 (ǒu chéng)

少年易老学难成，
一寸光阴不可轻。
未觉池塘春草梦，
阶前梧叶已秋声。

Zhuxi (1130—1200)

Composed by Accident

Youth is easy to grow old,
  but learning is difficult to achieve;
So do not waste an inch of time
  and let it lightly go.
Before I can feel the dream
  of spring grass in the pond;
The leaves of firmiana in front of steps
  rustled in the autumn wind.

翁卷 (1163—1245)

乡村四月

绿遍山原白满川，
子规声里雨如烟。
乡村四月闲人少，
才了蚕桑又插田。

Wengjuan (1163—1245)

The Village in April

The plains and mountains are green, the paddies shine,
 brightly with the sky,
The cuckoo calls, and veils of rain
 drift through the steamy air.
In April few are idle here,
 the village must prepare;
Just when the silkworms have been fed,
 rice-sowing time comes by.

叶绍翁 (1194—1269)

游园不值

应怜屐齿印苍苔,
小扣柴扉久不开。
春色满园关不住,
一枝红杏出墙来。

Ye Shaoweng (1194—1269)

Visiting a Garden but Denied Entrance

Perhaps my wood clogs worry him,
　　that they might mark his moss;
A while I knock the old board gate
　　but it still blocks the way.
But still the garden can't contain
　　the colors of the spring;
Outside the wall an apricot
　　extends a crimson spray.

张俞（不详）

蚕妇

昨日入城市，

归来泪满巾。

遍身罗绮者，

不是养蚕人。

Zhangyu (Unknown)

The Silkworm Girl

She went to town to sell silk yesterday;

Tears soaked her handkerchief when she returned.

The rich folks' bodies there were dressed in silk,

But silk is not for those who raise the silkworm.

志南（不详）

绝句

古木阴中系短篷，
杖藜扶我过桥东。
沾衣欲湿杏花雨，
吹面不寒杨柳风。

Zhinan（Unknown）

A Quatrain

That rain shade boat is moored beneath
    sheltering ancient trees;
My old quinoa stick helps me
    cross the bridge to the east.
Apricot flowering season now,
    rain wants to soak my clothes,
This breeze from the willows
    will not chill my face.

卢梅坡（不详）

雪梅·其二

有梅无雪不精神，
有雪无诗俗了人。
日暮诗成天又雪，
与梅并作十分春。

Lu Meipo (Unknown)

Snow and Plum Blossom (No. 2)

Without a snowflake by the bloom,
    Plum blossom has no soul;
If there is snow without a poem,
    a human is not whole.
It's snowing now at dusk, and I
    conjure to make verse sing;
Plum blossom and the snow combine
    to make a perfect Spring.